Mind Power

Mind Power

Change your thinking, change your life

2nd edition

JAMES BORG

PEARSON

Harlow, England • London • New York • Boston • San Francisco • Toronto • Sydney
Auckland • Singapore • Hong Kong • Tokyo • Seoul • Taipei • New Delhi
Cape Town • São Paulo • Mexico City • Madrid • Amsterdam • Munich • Paris • Milan

Pearson Education Limited
Edinburgh Gate
Harlow CM20 2JE
United Kingdom
Tel: +44 (0)1279 623623
Web: www.pearson.com/uk

First published in Great Britain in 2010 (print)
Second edition published 2014 (print and electronic)

Pearson Education is not responsible for the content of third-party internet sites.

ISBN: 978-1-292-00450-1 (print)
        978-1-292-00455-6 (PDF)
        978-1-292-00719-9 (eText)
        978-1-292-00454-9 (ePub)

British Library Cataloguing-in-Publication Data
A catalogue record for the print edition is available from the British Library

Library of Congress Cataloging-in-Publication Data
A catalogue record for the print edition is available from the Library of Congress

10 9 8 7 6 5
17

Cartoons: Bill Piggins

Print edition typeset in 9.75 pt Janson Text LT Std by 30
Print in Great Britain By Henry Ling Limited, at the Dorset Press, Dorchester DT1 1HD

NOTE THAT ANY PAGE CROSS-REFERENCES REFER TO THE PRINT EDITION

Dedication

To the hundreds of people who have revealed their thoughts and experiences, some of which manifest themselves in the pages of various chapters.

Also to the readers who are able to change their thinking and experience a more fulfilling personal and working life.

Contents

About the author

James Borg spends part of his working time as a business consultant and coach and also conducts personal development and business skills workshops covering memory improvement, persuasion, body language awareness and 'mind control'.

With a profound interest in the workings of the human mind, he developed memory techniques at an early age which eventually established him as a 'memory expert'. After becoming interested in magic, he later specialised and performed in the branch of the art known as 'mind magic'.

He's spent a lifetime observing the 'mind-body' connection and went on to study the various mind 'therapies' which result in thinking and behavioural change and from which he developed his 'mind control' workshops. His early interest in cinema – and also the performing arts – resulted in his research into the power of body language and its correlation with successful and effective communication in a person's personal and working life.

Influenced by an academic background in economics and psychology, his knowledge was honed in a career that spans the spectrum of advertising, sales, marketing, work psychology, training and journalism. He appears on BBC radio and contributes to national newspapers and magazines on the subject of consumer affairs, body language and business and communication skills. In 2009 he was chosen as a *Harvard Business Review* contributor. He still finds time to pursue travel and sports journalism which he became involved with early on in his career.

He is also the author of the Number 1 international bestseller *Persuasion* and the award-winning bestseller *Body Language*, the other two books that form the 'trilogy'.

Acknowledgements

Text

Quote on page 232 from 'Winning? It's all in the mind', *The Times*, 04/02/2010, © *The Times* and 4th Feb 2010/nisyndication.com.

Picture credits

The publisher would like to thank the following for their kind permission to reproduce their photographs:

Page 16: Science Photo Library Ltd / Jacopin; 20: used by permission from James N. Arrington; 38: Alamy Images / Dennis MacDonald; 61: Rex Features / Miramax / Everett Collection; 142: used by permission from James N. Arrington; 209: Alamy Images / Oredia; 233: Getty Images / Norman Potter / Central Press; 234: Corbis / Ben Radford; 253: Rex Features / Snap; 254 (top): Alamy Images / Moviestore collection Ltd; 254 (bottom): Rex Features / Everett Collection; 256: Rex Features / Everett Collection.

Every effort has been made to trace the copyright holders and we apologise in advance for any unintentional omissions. We would be pleased to insert the appropriate acknowledgement in any subsequent edition of this publication.

If there's a faith that can move mountains, it's the faith in your own mind power

'... for there is nothing either good or bad, but thinking makes it so'

William Shakespeare

Introduction

Can there be anything more important than our thoughts? Our thoughts create our reality. The quality of your thinking determines the quality of your life.

Thinking is something that is involved in everything that we do; something we engage in every day of our lives. Yet it's something most of us take for granted. Our mind is in use all the time, but most people don't give a thought (!) to their thinking process. There can surely be no other topic as important as this, as it is at the heart of everything we do. Oh, there is just one I should mention as more important – breathing.

What's this book about? It's about achieving emotional well-being and success in your personal and professional life by taking control of your thoughts and using this innate mind power of yours to change your attitudes and behaviour.

You'll have a 'blueprint' to free you from the tyranny of thoughts that limit your achievement – in *all* aspects of your life – and to show you how to replace these with a mind-set that puts you in charge. To take back control. The aim of this book therefore is to be thought-provoking (a noble aim, for a book about thinking!) and to raise an awareness within you of how you're perfectly able, with the power that you have, to control your thoughts instead of being controlled by them.

After all, it is only your mind that can propel you to success – *or* hold you back. **So to change your life all you have to do is change your thinking**. We start with the underlying 'bedrock' of beliefs and attitudes that we all hold. These drive our thinking and many of them are self-limiting in their nature.

I've been studying the mind for hundreds of years now (okay, it just *feels* that way). At an early age as I tried to push the boundaries of what a youngster (this one) could remember, it seemed to alter what we now know as the brain's 'neural pathways' so that it appeared that 'the more you remember, the more you remember'. Pretty soon reciting multiplication tables from 2 to 300 and other mental calculations was becoming much easier, as was remembering names, lyrics of pop songs and much more. All of this through 'pushing' the mind to go further and further with mental calculations.

My interest in magic – purely coincidental – took me further into the wonders of the workings of the mind, since magic targets the human brain. There was an even more 'synchronistic' direct connection as I specialised in that branch of the art known as 'mind-magic'.

Filling in time between studies and then occasionally performing, now and again, while I was in employment, my act (flatter myself with the term!) was called *The Mind and Magic of James Borg*. What was interesting was that most people found the 'mind' part really fascinating. Mind-reading, 'mind control' and anything to do with the mind seems to hold great interest for most people.

So I hope this book about the mind will enlighten you. If you take just one or two ideas that strike a chord and lead you to a more fulfilling life, then it's mission accomplished. As we progress through our journey of the mind we'll take a look at how all of us *are* what we think. How our beliefs and behaviour have defined us. We'll see how to change our viewpoint of things using the *MindControl* model which I've used in coaching, in workshops – and on *myself* over the years! This draws upon the principles of Rational Emotive Behaviour Therapy (REBT) which took its core philosophy from the writings and teachings of philosophers and ancients stretching back more than 2,000 years.

I'm 'standing on the shoulders of giants' who, over the ages, have stressed the importance of correct thinking. From the stoic philosophers like Socrates who told us that '*the unexamined life is not worth living*' and Epictetus who said '*what concerns me is not the way things are, but rather the way people think things are.*' Shakespeare rightly observed that '*there is nothing either good or bad, but thinking makes it so*'. The line extends over the centuries through to Norman Vincent Peale with his emphasis on the power of positive thinking, and more recently to the American psychotherapist Albert Ellis, the creator of REBT, which was so ground-breaking and successful it was taken up by many and led to the formulation of cognitive therapies.

So it's obvious that human beings haven't changed that much over the millennia. We still suffer from the same mental afflictions caused by an uncontrollable mind.

But does it have to be that way?

Stress is a feature of modern life and no one can say with any conviction that it doesn't touch them. A life that is trouble-free is an illusion. Fear and anxiety grip us all and we'll look at ways of recognising and tackling the thoughts that give rise to these emotions. Anger is one of those negative emotions that takes a toll on us both mentally and physically and managing this affliction is a prerequisite for well-being, so we'll look at ways to do this.

Just as you are what you *think* – you are what you *remember*. We'll take a stroll down the 'neural pathways' of your brain and look at how we store memories and see how your mind can power up those brain cells to remember more. Finally, we'll take a look at how – armed with our new way of thinking – we can look to our dreams and set about making things happen. The only difference in you will be a changed set of *beliefs* and *attitudes*. A magical 'ripple effect' from your changed cognitions.

The power of wise quotes to turn a person's life around is immense. I've interspersed a few in the following pages. You may want to commit one or two to memory or to perhaps write them down and refer to them from time to time.

I'm grateful to the hundreds of people who were prepared to share their 'thinking' with me – which was very enlightening – and also for contributing many anecdotes relating to their experiences, successes and failures in everyday life. To all of you, I say – your secrets are *not* safe with me! No, seriously – I have merely recounted some of the thoughts and instances that were contributed by some (obviously respecting anonymity).

The fact that so many of you were able to recognise that it was 'faulty' or 'negative' thinking that has held you back in life and that you found the *MindControl* model to be an eye-opening way of looking at things in the future, was gratifying. Equally, those of you that recounted how a resilient attitude and a more 'positive' thought process – after a lot of practice – have enabled you to achieve good and great things, was even more gratifying.

I've tried to strike a balance with depth, scientific research (free of jargon) and the real world. If you take away just a handful of ideas from this book that enables you to improve the way you think – and change your life for the better – my work will have been done. My inspiration in writing this book – as with the other two books in the 'trilogy' – is to *inform*, *educate* and *entertain*.

Your past, present and future are moulded by your thoughts. Remember – **your thinking is your life's autobiography**. So let's start writing the pages . . .

– James Borg

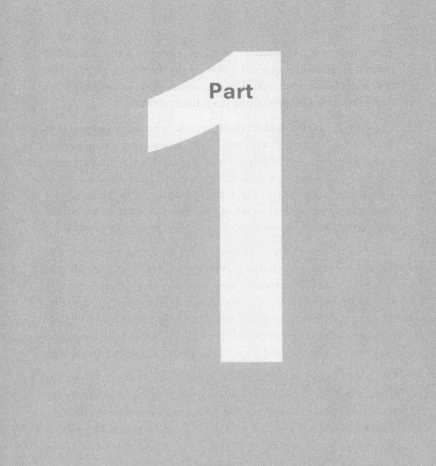

Part

1

It's the 'thought' that counts

Chapter

'You are today where the thoughts of yesterday have brought you and you will be tomorrow where the thoughts of today take you.'

Blaise Pascal

You *are* what you think

Did you know that on average we think around 60,000 to 80,000 thoughts every day? Staggering, isn't it? This means that the quality of our thoughts is responsible for how we feel and behave.

That inner dialogue in your mind is responsible for your lifetime's autobiography. Your thinking can propel you to success – or hold you back. So to change your life all you have to do is – change your *thinking*.

Do you control your mind? Or does your mind control you? When you recognise that it is *you* that holds the reins, all things are possible.

The way you feel on a day-to-day basis is determined solely by how you think. As far as your own life is concerned, it's make or break. No two ways about it; life's a battle – in varying degrees – for all of us. We face disappointments, worries, frustrations, financial problems, talk of impending doom on the state of the planet, not to mention the trauma of dealing with that other 'natural disaster' – human beings.

Although it is part of the human condition that we should naturally blame other people or our particular life 'script' for *making* us angry, stressed, sad, disgusted, anxious or whatever, in truth it's our *thoughts* that dictate how we feel and determine our subsequent behaviour.

You become what you think about – misery, pain, problems, love, kindness, hope? The answer to this question will, to a large extent, determine how you are going to feel.

How we cope with these everyday challenges and how troubled we become is purely down to the way we think about the situation. Through what 'filter' do we see the world?

To put it simply, if we're unable to change other people and our particular life situation we can at least change something that's within our **control**. We can use *mind power* – we can change the way we *think*, which in turn changes the way we *feel* about a situation.

So powerful is this neglected technique that it goes back to ancient times. Over the centuries the mantle was picked up by philosophers and other great thinkers. More recently – just over 50 years ago – the clinical psychologist Albert Ellis helped to raise awareness of the importance of changing unhealthy 'negative' thinking with his Rational Emotive Behaviour Therapy (REBT). My own studies in social and cognitive psychology were made all the more interesting through studying Ellis's techniques (so powerful that they paved the way for today's hugely successful cognitive therapies).

We're fortunate that since the nineties we know so much more about the brain. We know that it's the growth of the connections between our neurons (brain cells) that is responsible for the growth of the brain. The more that the brain is used and 'tested' the more those neuron connections get stronger and multiply, forming even more connections. These important findings have revolutionised our understanding of how **the mere act of 'thinking' changes the brain**. You may have heard the term 'plasticity' in relation to how our experiences mould the brain.

Can there be anything more important than our thoughts? Thinking is something that is involved in everything that we do, something we engage in every day of our lives. Yet it's something most of us take for granted. Our mind is in use all the time but most people don't give a thought (!) to their thinking process. Yet there can surely be no other topic as important as this, as it is at the heart of everything we do.

Just think about it. Look around you. Everything that you see began as a thought in somebody's head. The design of that chair; the cover of that book; that alarm clock; the laptop that allows you to be away from the office or home. Let's delve a little further into 'bigger' things: that computer (that spawned the aforementioned laptop); the invention of that communication medium, the telephone; taking the 'landline' for granted, the thought of a more 'mobile' device was pondered. What about the television over there? A product of the thought that the original miraculous cathode ray tube could be advanced to a flat screen. That aeroplane that's able to effortlessly rise to 30,000 feet . . .

I think the point's been made. All human endeavours in the fields of major inventions, medical advancements, nutritional discoveries, engineering, architecture, business – everything started out as a thought in someone's head.

Furthermore, they chose to have the vision to pursue it rather than take the easy option of: 'it'll never work; it's a ridiculous thought; I haven't got the confidence to . . .; things are okay as they are; others will laugh . . .; it can't be done.' And what about us as individuals? 'I'm not good at that sort of thing . . .' and so on.

As I stated earlier, the mind can propel us to do wonderful things or hold us back relentlessly.

Control your mind or *it* controls you

So we are all the product of what we think. From second to second, minute to minute we produce a running commentary in our head that will ultimately dictate an *action* or *intention* as well as a *feeling*.

The important question is this:

> **Do *you* control your mind?**
> **Or do you let your mind control *you*?**

Since your thoughts produce a feeling you may have been silently deluding yourself, for most of your life, that *you can't help the way you feel.* Tune in now, please, for the world's best-kept secret – we all have the power to change the way we feel. It's called mind power. And it's at your disposal.

This mind of ours that produces a particular feeling is benevolent enough to give us the power to enable us to *change* that feeling. Confused? Of course you're entitled to be. But think of it this way for a moment: **you are not your mind.**

As proof of this consider the fact that you are able to *watch* your mind.

When you're not with anybody and you're left with your own 'internal chatter', start watching your thoughts as they drift in and out of your head. Sit back for just two minutes and listen to your dialogue – keep a watch on it as a passive observer. Don't comment on the thoughts – just observe them – you're looking at them as an onlooker. Also notice whether you're being drawn in to accept some of the negative thoughts that might have popped into your head.

Well, what gems did the mind throw at you while you waited for that interminable two minutes to pass? Was it something like this (true example)?

'Mmm, ceiling needs a new coat of paint . . . is that a spider over there? . . . What time did I say I'd meet up with Natasha . . .? I suppose she'll look fantastic after two weeks in the sun . . . my skin's so dry and blotchy . . . that air conditioning makes such a racket . . . I'll never look glamorous like Natasha . . . this room's so poky . . . suppose I'll have to get to the dry cleaner's today . . . hate that new lady on the counter . . . where did I put that ticket? . . . wonder if those two minutes are up yet . . .?'

Assuming you were able to relate the thoughts that occupied your mind, you've just proved that you are *outside* of your mind.

You were *watching* your thinking. Therefore *you* **have the power to control your mind** (if you put your mind to it) – instead of **letting your *mind* control you.**

Recognition of this one simple fact could completely change the lives of millions of people. Yet it's not something that's become mainstream enough to have permeated society as a whole, except for those lucky people that have recognised the 'duality' of the capacity of the human mind – and used it to great benefit.

These people simply stay vigilant with their own internal chatter, recognising that it will always be a precursor to an action or attitude (and hence feeling) and therefore try – whenever possible – to replace negative or self-defeating thoughts with more positive or upbeat ones.

My own personal introduction to this area came as a pre-teen when in a school holiday I found myself thumbing through a very old 'grown-up' hardback book with heavy text that went on and on for hundreds of relentless pages – all of them yellowed through age and damp – with that musty smell that reminded you of the holy grail of childhood fantasy, *The Book of Spells* (this was of course pre-*Harry Potter*!). Then I came across a powerful section relating to the way we can think about life. It had a profound effect on me then – and it still does today. It was a 'Eureka' moment. Effectively, this is what it was trying to convey:

'Whether you're an optimist or a pessimist, may not affect the outcome. It's just that the optimist has a better time in life.'

That was it for me – just a 'flick of the switch' to change a way of thinking.

Why, I thought, spend nervous energy engaging in *negative* thoughts when the **same** thought process could swing towards optimism (at no extra cost!)? To use a phrase that's in vogue at the moment – and very apposite – it was a 'no-brainer'.

This reinforced the idea that if we are solely responsible for 'manufacturing' the thoughts, then we are responsible (and able) for *changing* those very same thoughts. So the shift to a healthier, optimistic frame of mind didn't seem like an *impossible* task.

Of course what it amounted to was changing an entrenched habit. For most people, the expectation of disappointment, frustration, unhappiness and loss is used as a *coping* mechanism in life:

'I suppose it'll rain on Saturday for the barbecue.'
'I bet the trains will be delayed again.'
'I'll never get the hang of this accounting software.'
'I never win raffles.'
'She won't call me (after first date), you'll see.'

What is beyond doubt is that the more attention you give to pessimistic thoughts the worse you'll feel, since feelings *follow* thought. Suppose you were able to change your habitual way of thinking and philosophically 'reframe' your thoughts on the above:

'Hope the weather's good for the barbecue. If it rains, well, so be it – we'll have a good time whatever.'

'Let's hope the train's on time today.'

'This new accounting programme's frustrating but I'll crack it, I've only had two days of it.'

'Well, I've never had luck in raffles so far, but somebody's got to win.'

'She may get in touch – we seemed to get on well.'

Just changing your internal **self-talk** will have an effect on your mood and your physiology. There hasn't been a wholesale shift in the factual elements of the 'activities'. There's still a barbecue, a train, accounting software, a raffle and a date. What's changed is a *belief* about the circumstances relating to each event. We've flicked the switch from a pessimistic to a more positive outlook. A change of attitude. You *feel* better.

Of course you may come across people who seem to have been lucky in the gene pool and seem to have a naturally optimistic outlook. But when you talk to a lot of these people – as I have – you find that they have, at one point or another, made it a *choice*. They had to learn how to mould themselves into that psychological state and simply learnt to change the way that they thought about things. How they looked at life. Their attitude towards life, as for all of us, comes from one thing – their thoughts.

The point about pessimistic thinking is that it pervades your life generally.

It stops you:

- **from doing things;**
- **from putting yourself in the midst of opportunities;**
- **from making things happen.**

The first requirement is to acknowledge to yourself that you tend to – or maybe just occasionally – veer towards a negative/pessimistic view of life and situations. Then remember this very important point (the central message of this book):

> **You are what you think – your thoughts determine how
> you feel.**

A lot of scientific studies have since been conducted into the negative and positive outlooks on life. You'll have frequently heard, no doubt, about the twin factors of optimism and pessimism in conjunction with the so-called 'half-full' (*optimistic*) or 'half-empty' (*pessimistic*) glass viewpoint. In other words: which way do you view the contents of the glass, as an approach to how you see things in life?

Or as one humorist put it:

'I see it as the host trying to get me to leave the party early!'

'Flick of the switch'

Decades later, with much psychological research and brain study behind us, we can now say that as well as being the best choice, this 'optimism' often does affect the outcome in certain instances – as it changes your actions and feelings. This in turn makes you first:

- reach towards a 'goal'; and
- put yourself in more favourable situations to try and achieve it.

Of course the optimism won't ensure you pick the multi-million pound lottery ticket – but it may at least *make you go out and buy one*. (The number of 'pessimists' that complain about the lack of a lottery win . . . having never bought a ticket!)

As you'll see throughout the book, it's just that *'flick of the switch'* in your mind that will introduce you to a whole new way of thinking. Your quality of life will change immeasurably. We've all been used to the idea of physical exercise in order to maintain physical health. If we're aware – or are told – that the body is dysfunctional, we may attempt to do something about it.

*Thinking is not something that **happens** to you. It's something that you **do***

The mind seems to have taken a back seat. We're so resigned to the mental side of our lives, it's almost apathy: we think – accept the stressors that life throws at us – try and deal with them (or not) – complain about the world – and the cycle continues.

Just as we take action for our physical well-being, we should be doing the same for our mental well-being.

Why? **Because you are what you think**.

Whether it's your personal life or your working life, there's no question that satisfaction and success will come only when your thoughts are right.

How you think will determine what you *do* in the outside world and also determine how you *react* to 'what life throws at you' – your experiences, in other words.

Your brain is a pharmacy

Since you are what you think, we'll be looking at types of unhelpful and distorted thinking in the next chapter and the emotions they tend to generate. Since the purpose of this book is to help you to change your thinking you need to know how to control your thoughts. Therefore it will be helpful for you to know how your thought process begins and where it can take you.

If you understand something you're better able to control it – instead of allowing it to control you.

What's really exciting in the study of the mind and the brain is the continued development in the brain imaging machines that were introduced in the nineties. We can 'see' the thinking process as it happens.

If you remember only one thing after reading this book, please remember this: your brain is like a pharmacy; and it never closes, dispensing chemicals at all hours. Every thought you have produces a biochemical reaction – with some reacting more than others depending on the emotional intensity of the thought. The mind and body are inextricably linked. **Your thinking generates emotions that generate chemicals** – but some chemicals are there to *help* you and some will *harm* you (we'll be taking a look at these shortly).

Also, later on we'll be taking a look at stress/anxiety and anger in some detail. When we continually live with psychological stress the constant release of chemicals – from the emotions we are experiencing – takes its toll on our health over time.

As you'll see, these negative emotions along with a host of others that we experience every day, are responsible for releasing an onslaught of damaging chemicals that not only affect us 'in the moment' but linger long after. We're all familiar with becoming ill or having that feeling of 'unwellness' after we've experienced difficult times; when we've had to grapple with negative thoughts in response to a difficult situation (either real or imagined) and the consequent effect it has on our immune system.

Conversely, we also release good or 'positive' chemicals when we experience good thoughts, which generate positive emotions, and enhance our mental and physical state. These strengthen our immune system and its fighting capabilities.

How do we instruct this 'pharmacy' in the brain to dispense either good or bad chemicals? Simple – by how we choose to think.

This thinking is then engaged in a *feedback loop*:

- so the more negative thoughts you have, the worse you feel, which causes you to have *more* negative thoughts, then you feel even **worse**;

- the more positive thoughts you have, the better you feel, which causes you to have *more* positive thoughts, then you feel even **better**.

A cascade of 'good' or 'bad' chemicals are created in a feedback loop. (You can see how easily some people sink into depression when this process is at work.)

- Think good thoughts – generate good emotions – generate good chemicals – **feel good**.
- Think bad thoughts – generate bad emotions – generate bad chemicals – **feel bad**.

It's the mind–body connection at work.

How a thought forms (and what it looks like)

Everything starts with a thought.

What's important to know about your thoughts is that each thought produces electrochemical activity in your brain. How is this so? Well, our system is made up of two elements:

1. Nervous system (electrical)
2. Endocrine system (chemical).

Let's take a look at what a thought actually *is* and what it looks like. Your brain is comprised of neurons (or nerve cells), see Figure 1.1 – in fact there are around 100 billion of them, each of them looking like tiny trees that are constantly growing more 'branches' known as dendrites (we'll cover more of this when we look at memory). It receives its messages through these dendrites. The greater the number of these dendrites the more 'connections' there are with other cells, and the more accessible the thought. These branches are involved in the process of receiving and then consolidating all the information that is sent from your senses.

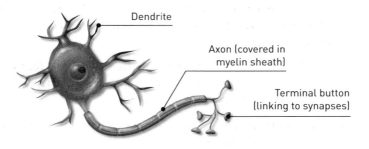

Dendrite

Axon (covered in myelin sheath)

Terminal button (linking to synapses)

Figure 1.1 A neuron (literally, a 'thought')

Just a quick word at this point. Because the brain's influence extends to the whole of the body and not just the head, these long tentacles of dendrites and axons (see above) protrude far and wide from the brain into nearly all areas of the body as they connect with our various muscles and organs forming what we term the nervous system.

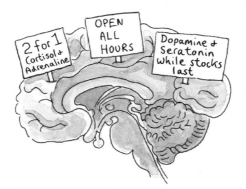

The partner to the nervous system, as mentioned earlier, is the endocrine system which is comprised of a number of small organs – the glands – that secrete various hormones into the bloodstream. We need to be aware, since we're interested in our thinking, of the adrenal glands as it is these glands that are responsible for the *fight or flight* response. Their 'master' is the 'pituitary gland' – a tiny gland about the size of a pea situated at the bottom of the brain. This is effectively the brain's pharmacy – open all hours – which is governed by the hypothalamus.

To simplify the electrochemical process: the neuron sends an electrical signal down the tube-like structure called the axon. When it reaches the end of the neuron that's when things start to get interesting for us humans. The neuron releases chemicals (neurotransmitters) into a very small gap known as a synapse. The chemicals do their best 'front crawl' in the sea of fluid in your brain until they see the comforting sight of the dendrite of another neuron. The receiving neuron reacts by 'firing' its own electrical signal.

With each thought you produce and the consequent feeling or emotion (reminder – emotions *follow* thought) there is an output of chemicals that circulate in the body through your bloodstream. These chemicals are called neurotransmitters. These thoughts that are generated in your mind and body originate in an area of the brain known as the limbic system and the outer part of the brain which is called the cortex.

Something that we'll be looking at in great detail is how thoughts are responsible for generating your *emotions*. Different emotions cause your brain to release a certain type of chemical. Essentially, the brain is a bit like a factory producing an output of different chemicals from its own built-in pharmacy – as we described it earlier – relating to the particular emotion that your body is experiencing.

In order to control and change our thinking we need to know how to change our reaction to our distorted way of thinking and feeling and take a different view of things.

Limbic system

It's helpful for you to know where the 'emotional centre' of the brain lies. It all takes place in the limbic system (Figure 1.2) – mentioned earlier – which is the part of the endocrine system

The mind is given to us, we are not given to the mind

that contains the important gland called the hypothalamus. It is this gland that is the 'head of pharmacy' as mentioned earlier and it takes decisions as to which chemicals to secrete based on a **thought** – or an **external** situation. Its other important function is controlling appetite.

It also has the task of stimulating the pituitary gland during the fight/flight response during periods of stress, fear, anxiety and anger (more of that in Part 2).

It's important to know that the hypothalamus dispenses chemicals **in response to your thoughts**. So when you change your thoughts from negative to positive, it acts accordingly. Also in the limbic system are the hippocampus, amygdala and thalamus which play an important part in interpreting whether we feel calm and relaxed or whether we are about to face a situation of 'threat' that requires the stress hormones to be activated throughout the body.

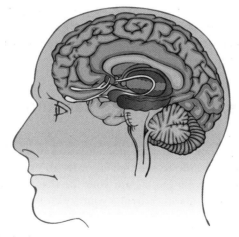

Figure 1.2 The limbic system

Some of these neurons are responsible for our state of happiness – the much-touted endorphins that are released by the brain when you feel pleasure. Equally, there are the less discussed chemicals that are produced by this factory when you are experiencing thoughts of unhappiness, fear, stress, guilt, depression, anger and other 'toxic' emotions. So your emotions – generated by your thoughts – are responsible for whether your body is releasing chemicals that *enhance* your well-being or whether they are *harmful* and contribute to health problems in your mind as well as your body.

Just a word on your negative thoughts before we proceed. As we'll touch upon later, the purpose and the aim of this book is to *reduce* your negativity – **not eliminate it completely**. We know that sometimes we will naturally have negative emotions in situations when it is appropriate and necessary in order to redress an immediate problem. We may experience anger when we're railing against injustice. Or we may experience fearful thoughts if there's impending danger or another threat to our well-being.

It's now firmly established that the mind and body are inextricably linked. To put it simply: the quality of your thinking is responsible for your emotional and physical state. So all your thoughts and emotions – whether they are positive or negative – are linked.

Thoughts: the good, the bad and the ugly

When I talk of 'flicking the switch' it's a change of mind-set so that you're looking at the same situation in a different way. I hope you'll be able to see that in order to experience a better and more satisfying life it's not your life that has to change. It's the thing that you can control – your style of thinking.

If I had to pinpoint the most surprising thing that I have discovered during workshops and conversations with people it is this:

- the majority of people believe that thinking is something that **happens** to them;
- rather than something they are **doing**.

The important point about this is that because it's something that you are actually responsible for, the *control* lies with you.

Since this is the misapprehension that I've discovered over the years from the majority of people that I've come across, I'm going to assume that it's a view that you, too, may have always taken (with apologies to those of you that are lucky enough to have already discovered the distinction and reaped the dividends in your life already).

With tens of thousands of thoughts a day just appearing and disappearing, some taking hold and going down a pathway, spiralling and multiplying, small wonder that we may think that thinking is an activity that just 'happens' and is foisted upon us.

> **The trouble is it's not usually the good thoughts that tend to occupy much of our thinking: it's mostly 'the bad and the ugly'.**

We all know people who may have money, a glamorous or exciting job, car of their dreams, husband/wife or boyfriend/girlfriend of their dreams (or husband/wife *and* boyfriend/girlfriend!), wonderful house. Yet, this doesn't necessarily equate with their sense of well-being. They don't have that feeling. Their thinking does not equate with their material and life circumstances. They may spend their time thinking about what they *don't* have, rather than what they *do* have.

We are thinking all the time – a simple statement but not something of which most people are necessarily aware. Because it's an activity that we're engaged in all the time, it's very easy to forget this simple fact. Yet it's so important. Why? **Because it manifests your feelings**.

The way you feel at this very moment has been determined by your thoughts. It's an ongoing process and it happens at an astronomical rate. Your thoughts and the translation into how you feel occurs in a matter of seconds, such that you're almost oblivious to it. I can't begin to tell you the number of people that I've encountered who are more than a little perturbed that it took them so long to *realise* that thoughts and feelings go together.

You cannot have a feeling **without** a thought.

Just a little experiment to demonstrate this:

1 Would you try to feel **sad** – without thinking some saddening thoughts.

2 Would you now try to feel **angry** – without thinking some thoughts that generate anger within you.

3 Would you now, finally, try to feel **guilty** – without thinking of thoughts that generate guilt within you.

Wasn't possible, was it? We're simply unable to *feel* emotions without the corresponding thinking to generate it. Now that we know this it means that we can be introduced to the world's best-kept 'secret'.

Your thoughts are responsible for your emotions.

- Optimistic and upbeat thoughts – we get optimistic and uplifting emotions. We feel good.

- Pessimistic and negative thoughts – we get pessimistic and downbeat emotions. We feel bad.

Which ones should we aim for? No need to think of an answer to that.

You cannot have unhappiness in your life, therefore, **unless** you have pessimistic thinking. It's the feeling that follows from this thinking. So this explains how we can see two people with almost identical adverse circumstances and one person responds in a healthier way than the other person. Purely because of the way that they *choose* to think about their circumstances.

It's only a thought, it can't hurt you

As I hinted at earlier, most of the people walking around you are totally oblivious to the fact that their feelings are coming from their own thinking. It's not even the events or situations that are causing the feelings. It's their reaction to situations that involves thoughts that generate these feelings.

We'll have to get this straight from the start: **you create your own thoughts**. Therefore if you're thinking depressing, or fearful or guilty or angry thoughts, you are actually hurting yourself. Nobody else is doing it to you. It's self-inflicted. I know when I point this out to people, after an automatic initial resistance, they begin to realise that it's absolutely true.

The power that exists is with your own mind; it is you who are the creator of your thoughts, so the power of 'ejecting' unhelpful thoughts is down to you.

Of course life will always be spent dealing with the cut and thrust of painful and negative thoughts no matter how successful you will be in thwarting most of them. As you realise they are merely thoughts in your own head, you'll develop a resistance to the feelings that previously accompanied this negative thinking. You'll recognise their true identity and watch them pass by instead of dwelling on them unhelpfully.

What about your opinions about yourself? We're talking about self-esteem, a term that you no doubt come across all the time. Your own thoughts relating to yourself are of course merely thoughts. *They are not real.* If you believe fervently that they are an accurate description of who you are, then you will conduct your life based on *your* assessment of your own strengths and limitations. How many opportunities have you shied away from because of your own self-imposed 'thinking errors'? (We'll talk more about these later.)

Your thoughts do not have the power to hurt you – unless you give them power.

Have you ever had the experience of being somewhere and having a great time – maybe in a restaurant with others – and feeling generally good about yourself and the world. Then, out of the blue, something you *see* or *hear* brings up a memory from the **past**, and in almost a split second you can go from feeling good to feeling depressed or frightened or angry.

If you follow that train of negative thought that came out of nowhere – being the controller of your own thoughts – it leads to more of the same type of thoughts and the spiral begins. Suddenly you're off on a journey of despair – and you haven't even left the restaurant. By becoming aware of our thoughts – and it's a habit that will take time to change – you'll gradually learn how to let the thoughts go. It's up to you. It's only a thought, it can't hurt you.

Of course if you're unaware that it's *you* who are the one responsible for your own pain, the process just carries on throughout your life. That's the case for the majority of us humans. It's hard to believe at first – after a lifetime of habitual thinking – that our own thinking has been the cause of a lot of our own suffering; that we've created our own pain.

The mistaken belief that thoughts are actually *real* can lead to that downward spiral of further negative thinking. Being not real, as such, they can't hurt you. When you finally realise that we are not talking about 'reality', but merely thoughts, you will find that you can bid them goodbye and therefore not suffer these adverse feelings.

Thoughts come. Thoughts go. *That's how it should be.*

As Jane makes her way to work in the morning her senses register a parked car with its window left open and then flit the next second to a thought about how green the next door neighbour's lawn looks; a cracked paving stone is registered next and then the next thought that pops into her head is that *if* the trains are delayed again due to signal failure:

'I'll miss the meeting – manager (Andrew) will be annoyed – everybody will think I'm irresponsible – he'll ask someone else to handle the client – probably Simon – they'll try and force me out of the job – I'll have a row with Mrs. Potter in human resources – she'll be wearing that awful magenta twin-set – I know she'll incite me to hit her – they'll have to restrain me after the tussle – pull me by my hair – my skirt will split – security will be called – they'll ask me to clear my desk – Mrs. Potter will press charges – I'll end up in court – maybe spend some time inside – sharing a cell – that awful prison gown – I couldn't eat with those other inmates – I'm not exercising in that yard – those showers – they smuggle knives – one phone call a day – I just couldn't stand it – I'd have to . . .'

Whoa, whoa . . . this sounds like a late-night B movie. That's exactly what we do, though. Construct mini-movies in our head at breakneck speed.

Just think: if the next thought after '*if the trains are delayed again* . . .' had been perhaps something neutral like, '*I must try that crayfish and rocket sandwich today*', that negative spiral of thoughts could have been nipped in the bud.

You can only think one thought at a time

Taking attention away from one thought and on to another will dispel the previous one. It sounds like an obvious statement but it's remarkable how many people – until it's pointed out – are not aware that:

you can only think one thought at a time.

To continue with an unhelpful negative train of thought is a slippery slope of despair as it often does not end there. Quite often, even after we've finished production on a particular 'movie', because we've started this imaginary downward spiral, we then continue on the same path of *more* negative thoughts. A new mini-movie takes shape after the curtains are down on the previous one. It's in the nature of the human mind that when we're in an unhappy state of mind all that we generate are thoughts of negativity. That's why it is so important to catch a line of thinking – to observe it in other words, and be aware of it – and prevent it from taking hold.

If we give no importance to a thought and focus our attention on something else, the thought *disappears*. The more attention you give to a particular thought the more prominent it becomes and the more 'scenes' you enact, as in the case above, which resulted in *custody* rather than *crayfish*.

We do not have that much control over:

● the *content* of our thoughts.

They just come and go as our senses pick up information through our consciousness. We have to control:

● how we *assess* the thoughts.

And take them for what they really are. Just that – thoughts and not reality.

Watch your thoughts

So the key is to actually watch your thinking rather than getting caught up in the vortex of continuous thoughts that go on and on, making you feel bad about a situation or your life in general. Recognise that your thoughts are not real – they are imaginary. They were conceived by you. And thoughts – whether they be positive or negative – gain momentum only through energy. Your energy. That is fine when you're using this to pursue a *positive* thought ('I'm going to train to be a Pilates teacher – and I'm going to be one of the best . . .') because your energy and attention will try and make this happen.

The same energy can be devoted in a *negative* way ('I'd like to have trained to be a Pilates instructor – but I don't think I've got the discipline – I've never been comfortable in any kind of speaking situation – I'd probably have to wear a leotard – shows up the bulges – the instructor I had last year had a perfect figure – maybe there are too many instructors around anyway – I'd have to talk to a class of many people – I remember 25 years ago I once gave a disastrous talk at a meeting . . .'). After this internal dialogue the person feels bad. Since feelings follow thought – she's just made herself feel miserable. Nobody even had to do it to her!

The point about your thinking is that once a thought pops into your head and you've observed it, you can then take control and do something about it. In the case of the potential Pilates teacher, if she'd have watched her thinking, she could have stopped her thoughts at 'but I don't think I've got the discipline'. She's rationalised – whether true or not – that there may be a motivational problem. Now's the time to stop, instead of dwelling on a cascade of further self-defeating thoughts. Our future teacher carried on down towards the spiral and introduced a whole array of further points to make herself feel bad. When we stepped out of 'her mind' she was just about to regale *herself* with a disastrous experience from her past – 25 years ago – relating to public speaking. All of it in the mind.

Stopping negative thoughts in time is the way you gain control. Just a reminder again – *you* control your mind, your *mind* doesn't control you. Yet, sadly the latter is the way that it is for most people. But you can break out of this trap as you gradually change those stubborn thinking habits.

When you realise that you are able to step back and be critical about what you are thinking – which path you are about to go down – it gives you immense power over your mind. You can *choose* not to think in a destructive or negative way. Why are we spending so much time discussing this negative and sabotaging style of thinking? It's because, as I said earlier, this is the bane of the human condition. It's what we do best. We find it easier to dwell on adverse thoughts rather than more positive and uplifting ones. The 'spiral' is usually downwards rather than upwards. Anxiety, worry, depression, anger, guilt – these are all natural bedfellows for our active minds, as one thought leads to another unhelpful thought. By realising that the thoughts came from within you and are not the result of any external event or circumstance you will know that the solution will come from within you. **It is you who are doing the thinking so it is you who are responsible for changing your thinking**.

There's a phrase that I use to sum up the cause of and solution to your unhelpful thinking:

> **'Your thinking got you *into* this mess.**
> **It's your thinking that'll get you *out* of it.'**

Stop your thoughts

Because you've had a lifetime of dealing with thoughts that come in and out of your head every day, you probably have never considered that you are constantly receiving and 'tossing aside' thousands of these thoughts almost unconsciously.

Of course we would be unable to function if we 'processed' every minor observation/thought that came into our minds. We selectively focus on those that we consider important. For example, while you're wandering around in a department store you notice a shop assistant who reminds you of your niece – all well and good. But you decide to dwell on that thought because she's jogged your memory that your niece was taking her driving test later that month. You'd wanted to remember to send her a good luck card and you would have forgotten. So you hang on to that thought until you get to the second floor where they sell greetings cards. This was a thought that you held on to because it served a purpose. You were able to control the momentum of the thought.

If you were in the theatre watching a play and the lead character's dressing gown reminds you of your own threadbare imitation, your mind may go on its journey to the future and start to think, 'Nice colour, I must get a new one . . . I wonder whether . . .' and then you bring yourself back to the present and let the thought pass so that you don't lose track of the play.

So we're perfectly able to let thoughts come and go – providing we don't let them take hold of us.

This brings us to another important point. Many people I speak to are a little confused as to how you can – and whether the idea is to – prevent thoughts coming into your head in the first place. But as I mentioned earlier, the emergence and content of thoughts is something that just happens and there is not much we can do about that. What you *can* do something about is how you treat the thought when you've *had* it.

Your control over your thought happens **after** it's actually been formulated. So the member of the audience in the theatre can start to dismiss their thoughts about what type and colour of dressing gown and where to buy one – until after the performance! Just as we're able to postpone or reject that thought, we can do the same with unhelpful thoughts as well. There's no question that when we think negatively the hurt or bitterness or pain or suffering or worry or anxiety or guilt – all powerful emotions – is felt. We suffer rather than the other person – or the 'situation'.

You'll remember that we drew a fine distinction – that thinking is something that you actually do rather than something that happens to you.

If you analyse this then of course you will understand that if it's something that you are *doing* then the control lies with *you*. Alternatively, those people who are under the misapprehension that thinking just *happens* to them will be in a position of help-lessness. They think that they have to:

● entertain the particular line of thinking;
● and so get caught in an endless loop of thoughts.

It's only your awareness that will let you know which thoughts need to be acted on and which should be rejected.

A clear mind is better able to handle those thoughts that are genuine concerns or events that need to be acted upon. If you're constantly entertaining thoughts that shouldn't be given air-time then you're trapped in your own thinking and your mind is constantly in a muddle. Your stress levels will be high and your memory will be impaired (more about this in Chapter 4).

Coffee break . . .

 We think around 60,000–80,000 thoughts per day. Changing your self-talk has an effect on your mood and physiology.

 Everything that you see began as a thought in someone's head.

 You cannot have a feeling without a thought.

 Changing the way you *think* changes the way you *feel*, which changes your *behaviour*. We are all the product of what we think.

 If we are unable to change other people, or our particular life situation, then we must remember that our thinking is within our control.

 You can 'watch' your thinking, therefore you have the power to control your own mind – instead of letting it control you.

 How you think will decide how you *react* to what life throws at you.

 Your brain has its own built-in 'pharmacy'. Your thinking generates *emotions* that generate *chemicals* – some of these help you and some don't.

In your 'limbic system' the hypothalamus dispenses chemicals in response to your thoughts – when you go from positive to negative (or vice-versa) it acts accordingly.

The majority of people think that thinking is something that 'happens' to them rather than something they are 'doing'.

Your thoughts, and the translation of them into how you feel, occurs in a matter of seconds – so you're almost oblivious to them.

 'Flick the switch' – you can't have unhappiness unless you have *pessimistic* thinking. Equally, you cannot have happiness unless you have *optimistic* thinking.

 Your thoughts do not have the power to hurt you unless *you* give them power.

 We tend to suffer from the mistaken belief that thoughts are actually *real* – they are not reality, merely thoughts.

 The more attention you give to the negative 'mini-movies' in your head, the more 'scenes' you enact and the worse you feel.

 We may not have control over the *content* of thoughts, but we have control of how we *assess* them.

Chapter

2

'Old habits can't be thrown out the upstairs window. They have to be coaxed down the stairs one step at a time.'

Mark Twain

The power of 'distorted' thinking

Much research has been done since the 1950s in the area of negative thinking patterns that are adopted by most of the population – at one time or another. We'll take a look at some of the major ones that psychologists have identified.

So common are these 'distorted' thought processes that you may grimace if you recognise yourself as you look down the list. I know I did, the very first time I was introduced to these types of 'cognitive bias' when I was studying REBT (Rational Emotive Behaviour Therapy).

It's not always easy to recognise when you're engaging in this kind of thinking. The point is that whatever thinking people do engage in, they tend to assume that even if it veers towards the negative it is still rational. This is obviously the case in *some* instances – when your state of mind is healthy. But usually when we're saddled with a dysfunctional state of mind, the negative thoughts are *irrational* in nature.

The three-part thinking challenge

Challenge your thinking after considering this three-part statement:

1 Why assume thoughts about yourself and the world are *true*?
2 Remember that thoughts don't always reflect *reality*.
3 Distorting mirrors don't reflect the way you *really* look.

The Thinker (by Auguste Rodin)

When you begin to analyse your thoughts in a typical day (and as we noted earlier there are around 60,000 to 80,000 of them in a day) you'll become aware that a great deal of them are actually thoughts *about* the *original* thought.

So we have a thought and then start thinking about that thought . . . and then start thinking *about* the thought *about* the thought . . . and so on. Get the idea? (Can you see how the spiral of negative or depression-inducing thinking can just take over?)

- In effect what we often tend to do is have thoughts that are either engaged in **analysing** or **justifying** the *original* thought.

We've established that you are what you think. The brain spends much of its time rewiring all the various connections between your neurons. So it's constantly engaged in strengthening the ones you use and doing the opposite (weakening) for the ones you don't. What happens when you spend your life thinking in a distorted way? Exactly – you strengthen the neural pathways and make it much easier to find and navigate the distorted path.

Therefore you develop thinking habits that are automatic. Fine – if the thoughts are good, but not if you're going down a negative path. The problem is – you become an expert. An expert in distorted thinking! Not an accolade you particularly want!

The more the mind focuses on something the more it gets involved. In the case of 'distorted' or negative-type thinking if we try and repress the thought and supplant it with a healthier, positive thought, it doesn't work. **We need to let it go** – like a balloon on a string. It's enough to see it drift away into the atmosphere – thanks and goodbye. It's the fact that you are *aware* of a negative thought that is key. Why?

Because it means you have 'stepped back' and guessed its identity – it's just a thought. A thought is not necessarily a fact. When you gradually change your habits and start to develop an awareness of what a thought really is, you're on the way to self-empowerment. Because you're not making the mistake of *identifying* with it.

When you look at some of the different types of unhealthy and distorted thinking in which we engage, and how when we exercise the *MindControl* technique (next chapter) we can dispute their validity, you'll notice that self-awareness is the power that guides you.

The important thing is that these types of thinking form the core of the unhealthy thinking styles that prevent us from achieving a better life – in all areas. They are true distortions which can severely hold you back from doing things (as you've probably found out). After all, *you are what you think*.

As we become identified with our thinking habits we form neural pathways that lead us down this habitual thought path that results in damaging our confidence, limiting our performance and weakening our mental resolve.

So your thinking can be classified as distorted when, amongst other things, you:

- criticise yourself for past 'failures';
- doubt your abilities;
- fear future 'events';
- put yourself down;
- have an expectation of failure.

The point to remember is this (and please *do* remember it as it will form the foundation of your new way of thinking): it makes no difference how strongly you **believe** something – it doesn't make it true.

As we touched upon earlier, very few people are aware – that is, not consciously aware – of how their thinking is *affecting* their feelings. Just becoming an 'expert' in recognising the different types of thinking will gradually alter your automatic negative thoughts.

Just worth pointing out at this early stage: negative thoughts tend (rather like an irritating flying insect) to zoom into your mind, do the damage and then flit off again quickly, so that you hardly notice the 'bite' that's been left. Only later when you start experiencing the *feelings* do you notice that there's been an 'intruder' in your consciousness.

When unhelpful thoughts pop into your head you'll be able to instinctively put them into **one or more** of the categories that we're about to look at. This will enable you to be more *rational* and allow you to dispute your beliefs and consequently change how you feel. Again, it's not easy in the beginning. We're changing entrenched habits that have become part of your make-up.

Take a look at the following thinking distortions and:

1 After you've been through the whole list think about some 'distorted' thinking to which you may currently be subjecting yourself and place it into the relevant category.

2 Before you move on to *MindControl* in the next chapter, just attempt a healthier and more constructive internal dialogue with yourself to challenge this way of thinking.

Should/must (rigid way of thinking)

When we look at the way in which most of us exhibit distorted thinking there is quite often a belief that the world or situations or things or people 'should' or 'must' be a certain way (result: **anger** and **frustration**). Because this is such a common thinking pattern – which severely limits you in life – it merits a lot of discussion. It's also responsible for a lot of **guilt** in our lives.

Also in this category we can put 'ought' and 'have to'. These too will be very familiar to you.

Very few of us do not hold some rigid or inflexible beliefs. The world **should** be like this . . . other people **should** behave in this way . . .

There is no flexibility of thought – it's an absolute. These are rigid beliefs. To make matters worse, we apply them to *ourselves* – 'I should have . . .' done this or that . . . or be a certain way, causing us to experience guilty feelings and frustration.

Sounds like trouble brewing . . .

Be careful of the words you use at all times – in speech as well as thought.

- I should be earning big bonuses like those useless bankers.
- I should be married by now.
- I have to be more considerate about . . .
- They ought to notice when there's a long queue.
- I should be more appreciated by . . .
- I should have been more supportive.
- I must always be on time.
- I ought to have mastered this by now . . .
- I should have married Andrew, then I would have . . .
- She shouldn't be so suspicious . . .
- I should have achieved more in my life by now.
- I should be like the others in the office . . .

- They should have enough salt for the roads.
- I should never have let him . . .
- I should have trained as a lawyer and I could have been . . .

There are three things that tend to occur when you think in this way:

1 You enter a land of make-believe – forsaking *reality* – of how things 'should' be.

2 Precious time and emotional energy is expended on criticising or condemning whatever it is that is *violating* the 'should'.

3 The emphasis is on the problem and how *bad* you feel about it, rather than looking for a *solution*. Instead of making you feel motivated it tends to make you feel as though you're under pressure.

When we say to ourselves that taking path B – instead of path A, which we chose – would have been better because it would have led to 'this' instead of 'that', we're creating a reality that is entirely of our own fabrication.

Life being how and what it is, we set ourselves up for misery if we hold these rigid beliefs about how *people* should be, *things* should be and *we* should be. The problem is the stubbornness in the beliefs which can only lead to bad feelings.

The healthy approach to thinking is to eliminate the thought that things should or must be a certain way – we need to think more in terms of preferences. Beliefs will not cause a problem if we think of them as desires and realise that things do not have to unfold in a certain way. The healthy way of thinking – as opposed to demanding that situations should be different to how they are – is to *prefer*:

- that things should be a certain way;
- that people behaved in a certain way;
- that they treated us in a certain way;

whilst having the *flexibility* to cope when things don't happen this way.

It's back to word control. As they stand, all of the above 'should'-type statements place control *outside* yourself. To put it another way, the locus (or centre) of control is outside of you. The demands are almost like a critical parent or schoolteacher waiting to reprimand you if any of the statements are not adhered to. Can you identify with this? When you change the phrasing – and also your cognitions – you've brought the locus of control *inside* yourself. The result is less potential for distress now you're in control of the statement or demand, instead of it being in control of you.

Let's look at some of the examples above. First, we want to eliminate the 'should' from any statement. Then, having got rid of the emotive word, an important point: we have to change the way we think as well, in order to adopt a more flexible approach, so that self-talk gives the right feeling.

Avoid guilt, frustration and anger by 'reframing':

- I'd like to have achieved more by now (I must talk to HR about the possibility of . . .).

- It would be nice to be more appreciated by . . . (I might have to bring to John's attention the fact that . . .).

- It would be good if management noticed a long queue . . .

- I'd like to be earning big money like those bankers we've bailed out (I'm going to talk to those . . .).

- I'd hoped the trains would improve with the new owners . . . (I might have to think about getting an earlier one and leaving the office earlier).

- She'd be better off looking at last year's minutes instead of regarding it with suspicion . . . (let's e-mail . . .).

- It might be an idea to start a diet (I must check out that health club flyer I kept . . .).

This kind of talk creates less bad feeling and allows for the impetus to try and change things. The situation doesn't seem so hopeless. It's a subtle way of taking the emotion out of your system. Give up being a 'should' and 'must' victim and allow yourself to be creative in handling situations, to unleash positive energy and motivation and to free yourself of guilt.

We're switching from stick to carrot as you switch your mind to attaining a GOAL. Notice that in the revised way of thinking above, there's an action involved towards attaining an objective. But just to reiterate: as well as changing the rigid words you have to change your beliefs at the same time, otherwise you'll still end up feeling bad.

Pause for a few minutes: now make a little list of those *tyrannical* 'should'/'must' statements and put them in two categories:

1   Those that your mind has been manipulating you to attend to relating to **yourself** (for example, 'I should tidy my desk – I can't find anything, it's a tip. But I can't face it', 'I ought to tidy out the loft but there's so much other work to do at the weekends', 'I should be thinner'.) Do they make you feel guilty?

2   Those that are related to **external** events. Some will be long-standing, some may be more recent. ('They should answer the phone quicker', 'She ought to consider me for that promotion', 'Those builders should smile more – they're scaring the cats'.) Do they occupy a lot of your mental 'chatter'?

After you've made the list in the two categories take a long look at what you've written.

Apply a little disputing or questioning to the items on your list. Note that in reality it is our personal preferences that dictate this chatter rather an absolute law of the universe that says (using our examples) you have to 'tidy out the loft' or 'should be thinner' or that 'the builders should smile'.

Now that you know that, take a look at your list again, or when you have time to scribble out some of these 'demands' that you make. Make a note of every time you either voice or engage in self-talk that involves 'should/must/ought/have to'. Then challenge the way you've been speaking to yourself and see if there's a better way of phrasing some of these demands. For example:

'I think I'll make a start on decluttering the loft when Kate and Simon start school holidays – they can help me, if there's a bar or two of chocolate involved . . .'

(Less pressure than 'I should tidy out the loft'.) Also, look at those items on the list that are simply a case of you just being hard on yourself – ones that perhaps should be eliminated altogether, but are there in your mind through guilt or unease. For example:

'I must get in touch with Francoise – I really ought to.'

Dispute/challenge:

'I need to remind myself why I haven't been in touch with Francoise for over six months. If people are divided into "drains" and "radiators" – she's definitely become a "drain". She left me exhausted. And she kept forgetting things that we spoke about and was continually hogging the conversations. Why am I feeling guilty, for no reason? I don't want to get in touch with her again really – that's why six months have gone by already. The same things would happen again if we met up. And I'd end up feeling annoyed again.'

That's one off the list!

Your rational self-talk should help you to:

1 Concentrate the mind on looking for a *solution*.
2 Minimise the waste of *time* and draining of *energy* that you expend on complaining and fretting about the situation that violates the 'should/must/ought/have to' rules.
3 Get back to the 'real' world of how things *are* as opposed to 'should be'.

Just another point to consider. Quite often you'll observe – internally and externally – that there are 'should/must' statements that are 'packaged' in a different way in the form of questions. But they amount to the **same** thing. They affect your mind in the same way. Let's call these why can't? how could? why am I? why did? type statements. You ask yourself questions over and over again – questions that are irrelevant or fall into the category of ones that you have an answer to already – but you've developed a resistance in terms of accepting it.

'How could she be so insensitive as to say a thing like that?'
(True meaning: 'She *shouldn't* be so crass and rude.')

'Why can't I ever work out how to split the bill accurately?'
('I *should* be able to do simple adding up.')

'Why am I like this?'
('I *shouldn't* be like this and I'm not happy with the way I am/behave.')

'Why did that maître d' greet you and just ignore me?'
('He shouldn't ignore women. Trumped up chauvinist.')

Recognise these disguised forms of the same thing as they lead to the same route of negative emotions – challenge and use your rational self-talk and change of cognitions to rephrase these disguised should/shouldn't interpretations.

Overgeneralising

Negative formulations about life, other people, ourselves are drawn from limited experiences which may even have only happened *once* before. So you come to a conclusion about things, situations or people based on limited evidence from maybe just a single event. You formulate the idea that this is what *always* happens, all the time.

- You make an important mistake in the budget forecast in the report for the monthly meeting (first time it's happened) – so you're incompetent and you'll never be trusted anymore.

- You take the wrong exit at a roundabout so you're a hopeless driver.

- You forget to wash your little boy's sports kit so you're a terrible mother.

- The steak is tough so you're obviously a bad cook.

You'll also recognise this style of thinking if you just consider the words like **'never'**, **'always'**, **'the world is . . .'**, **'society's . . .'**, **'everybody . . .'**, **'every . . .'**, **'nobody . . .'**.

Have you thought or said (or heard somebody say) anything similar to the following recently?

'I *always* end up in the slowest checkout [at supermarket].'

'Those trains are *always* late since the new franchise took over . . .'

'Why does *everybody* stand at the ticket machine and then take ages to find their money.'

'Damn pigeons are *always* leaving a deposit on my new car [shame it's never when you're about to buy it!].'

'*People* are so selfish these days.'

'*Nobody* will trust me again after that idiotic mistake I made.'

'That's three boyfriends in as many months – all no-hopers. I'll *never* find anyone.'

I think it's fairly obvious that none of these is as extreme as they sound. But the fact is that whether you voice these or engage in self-talk (thoughts), it's unhealthy thinking. Designed to make you feel bad.

You can see how 'overgeneralising' about something leads to a perception of a situation being worse than it actually is in reality.

It's interesting that we tend to be quite severe with ourselves as we engage in self-talk and since we're talking to ourselves there's no 'referee'. But we should get into the habit – and as we noted earlier it takes time to change entrenched habits, especially thinking – of disputing our unhelpful thoughts. This comes with time after you learn to 'rewire' your brain so that it follows the pathway that steers clear of negative thoughts.

The idea of inviting such self-critical thoughts will gradually fade if you consider this: if you had a close friend in a similar situation to yourself, would you say those things to them?

Suppose you failed to mention something about yourself during an important interview and also, to make matters worse, were late because you left the instruction letter at home and had to go back from the station to get it. You didn't get called back for a final interview.

Your self-talk: 'How could I forget to mention that John Cameron, who used to be their PR director, was my boss at the last firm I worked for and said he'd be happy to talk on the phone with her? She was okay about me being late – I think. I know it put her out a bit. I'm such a fool. How could I forget such an important point. I should have left earlier as well. Then when I had to go back to pick up that letter, I still would have been on time. I really should prepare better. I'll never land another job at this rate.'

Imagine yourself saying to a friend: 'You're such a fool. How could you forget that? And you were late. Why didn't you leave earlier? You really should prepare better. You'll never get another job.'

How would that make them feel? Bags of self-esteem, unlimited confidence . . . supreme optimism for the future?

The truth is you'd be saying something that was the opposite, like: 'Look, you had a lot on your mind. I've often forgotten to say things during an interview – it's all that cortisol flying around in your system. We've all been late due to unforeseen circumstances – again it's not your fault. I'm sure you'll find something soon – economy's picking up.'

Don't believe
everything you think

So it's important to apply these principles to ourselves. Ask yourself – is that how I'd speak to somebody I cared about? Would it make them feel good or bad about the situation? You know the answer. *So talk to yourself in a more encouraging way and change your feelings.*

Pause: time to think.

Can you recall the last time you engaged in this kind of thinking? What effect did it have?

Labelling

Another distorted thinking habit is labelling. This can be when we attach a description to ourselves or to others. You'll know what I mean. You do it frequently. Before we get into the labels, it should be said that as human beings part of our inevitable make-up is that we do things that we regret, we make mistakes, fail to achieve what we go for, make bad decisions, criticise people – I'd better stop now, it's worse than I thought!

Again, the key to everything is our self-talk. When we concentrate on criticising our behaviour – 'That wasn't my best idea', 'I'll have to handle the Valentine's Day dinner differently next time', 'That was a mistake on my part' – that's okay. We're criticising an *isolated* incident that has no reflection on our worth as a person.

When we start using terms like 'failure', 'loser', 'stupid', 'hopeless' or 'incompetent', it can prove to be self-fulfilling as it discourages further activity. Action follows thought, remember? Language like this, when used about you by other people (and also by you in your own self-talk), can cause problems, as more and more studies prove – especially if a person is suffering from low *self-esteem*. This applies to other people as well as ourselves.

The labelling tends to trigger emotions such as shame, guilt, anxiety, self-loathing and even depression. As well as assigning terms to ourselves – even though of course it is absurd to define a complex person through isolated behaviours – we label other people.

So other people may be useless, inconsiderate, no good. 'The manager I work for, she's a real bitch.' This may fuel anger and resentment, leads to a waste of precious mental and nervous energy, and affects our interpersonal relations. What we ought to be doing is trying to separate a person's *behaviours* from the person as a whole. It's not the character of the person that is causing us problems usually, it's their thinking and/or behaviour. Only by recognising this can we feel motivated to try and improve the relationship by communicating in a different way.

Some labels may be a hangover from childhood days. They may have been attributed to you by other children or parents or other authority figures. Equally, you may have heard terms that stuck with you and you find yourself using them, if not on *yourself*, on other people.

I'll just list a few negative terms that you may find yourself using with regard to yourself or others:

Aggressive	Failure
Arrogant	Hopeless
Bitchy	Hysterical
Bossy	Immature
Chauvinist	Inferior
Crazy	Insensitive
Disgusting	Irresponsible
Lazy	Thoughtless
Petty	Troublemaker
Repulsive	Ungrateful
Selfish	Useless
Stubborn	Weak
Stupid	Worthless

It's important to remember that labels are abstractions – and inevitably inaccurate. When you label:

- yourself;
- other people;
- or events;

in a negative way, these emotionally charged words produce negative feelings that may stifle you and also steer you in the direction of engaging in adverse behaviour. Labelling another person as irresponsible, for example, may generate feelings of anger within you, and you may also receive reciprocal treatment from the other person.

You call your sister-in-law 'irresponsible' because she's twice left the front door key in the lock when you've loaned her the key. She remonstrates angrily the second time and points out that she was doing some shopping for you. The reason it happened, she points out, is because the first time she was distracted at the door as her mobile phone rang. The second time – well, she just forgot to take it out the door as she picked up the supermarket bags.

Emotionally laden labels applied to other people on the basis of one or two misdemeanours can cause friction. Is she really irresponsible, generally? Her actions may have been a little careless, but she objects to her whole being – her identity, in other words – assigned a label that marks her out as an irresponsible person.

Equally, we apply labels to ourselves. 'I'm worse than pathetic.' 'I'm useless.' 'These are the actions of a moron.' Statements like these, either as self-talk or voiced as a statement, often have a debilitating effect on the mind. Accept that you behaved in a pathetic way. Or performed a task in a sub-standard fashion. Or did something like a moron. *Single actions*. Separate what you did from the 'self'. Move on. If you don't, the mind can't work on improvement.

Personalising

You're probably very familiar with this one – it's so common and such an instinctive reaction. You take the blame for things that are not necessarily your fault even though they're not under your control. What somebody says or does is a direct reaction to *you*.

The result: repeated instances of feeling hurt and sad – and feeling guilty when it's not your fault.

- You bump into an acquaintance at the theatre in the interval of the performance: she's holding two glasses of wine. She says a cursory 'hello' while awkwardly holding the glasses and dashes off without saying much.

Your thoughts:	**'I've done something to offend her. She's normally very chatty.'**
Her thoughts:	**'I'd better get this wine to John. What a ridiculous queue. He'll think I've been treading the red grapes. If I don't put these glasses down soon I'm going to drop them – I need to get to the loo as well.'**

- The boss passes you in the corridor just as you're off to lunch (after his meeting with the finance director) and barely acknowledges you apart from a wry smile.

Your thoughts:	**'What have I done now? I was only ten minutes late this morning. I stay late most evenings. He's been to see Crawford over in finance. Maybe I'm in line for redundancy. That's why he couldn't look me in the eye.'**
His thoughts:	**'That meeting went on a bit. I bet they'll have run out of brie and cranberry sandwiches over the road now. I'll have to get a pasty from . . .'**

- Your friend Trudy arrives at your house: 'Hi, Amanda. House looks really nice and tidy today.'

Your thoughts: 'Is that a dig? Does she think it's untidy when she's been round in the past? I'll have to be careful in the future.'

Her thoughts: 'How nice and spotless the room looks when it's flooded with sunshine. And so tidy – unlike ours with John's papers, books and computer and printer cables everywhere.'

Remember that not everything that happens is a result of our 'imperfections' – it's not always about us. Jumping to conclusions as to why somebody is not as talkative with you on a certain occasion – as they normally are – can be something related to *them*. Harassed, worried about something, headache, toothache . . . the list is endless.

People with a strong tendency to personalise will *unnecessarily* spend a lot of their cognitive life embroiled with feelings of hurt and guilt which is often unfounded. And it can fracture relationships.

Blame

Unlike the previous thinking distortion – personalising – this style of thinking is the total opposite in that it's the fault of **other** people, circumstances, the world that something has happened or whatever problem has occurred. As a victim of the situation, the person's energy is spent on casting or apportioning blame rather than seeking a way to rectify or get over the problem.

If blame can be given over to someone or something else, then there is no need to analyse our own thinking or behaviour and see whether we may have contributed – or whether we may be too harsh in our interpretation. We avoid taking any personal responsibility:

- 'It's because of him that I decided to shout at the cashier.'
- 'She's ruined the entire holiday by doing that.'
- 'They've made me not want to do my job well by piling stuff on me.'
- 'He's single-handedly spoilt it for me.'

Self-blame

The opposite to the thinking style above, as you tend to take responsibility for things that are clearly not down to you.

- 'It's my fault. I chose the builders – they seemed all right. I got references.'
- 'I shouldn't have let Sue go to the shops. Then she wouldn't have lost her earring.'
- 'If I'd have got into work earlier, I could have prevented the flood.'

Magnification/filtering

This is probably very familiar to you – making mountains out of molehills by taking the negative elements of an occurrence and magnifying them – whilst filtering all of the positive elements – creating a distorted picture of events. You might speak as 'best man' at a wedding and give a good speech (that everyone enjoyed) but because you stalled for a while – you forgot the bride's mother's name – you feel it was a bad performance.

You organise a good conference at a hotel and everything goes to plan except there's a mix-up with the rooms and the MD has to wait half an hour before he and his wife get into their room. Consequently, your perception of the event is that it didn't run smoothly, despite the keynote speech and dinner being a great success.

All-or-nothing thinking

This type of thinking is characterised by a tendency to view things in extremes – either good or bad. This applies to ourselves, other people, events and situations. It is sometimes referred to as black-or-white thinking – there are no shades of grey or any middle ground.

- 'If I don't get straight As the whole thing's been a waste of time.'

- 'Either I lose eight pounds or this exercise regime has been a waste of time.'

- 'If we don't win the match it'll have been a waste of a Saturday afternoon.'

This rigid style of thinking can cause a lot of psychological stress. It can contribute to a lot of anxiety. Many people with 'perfectionist' type tendencies will think in this way and the high standards and goals that they set for themselves often spill over into all aspects of their lives.

If this all-or-nothing thinking dominates then a person's accomplishments and everyday experiences never live up to the unrealistically high standards they have set for themselves. The result is an inevitable reduction in self-esteem as the person experiences a negative self-image. This inevitably affects behaviour as it may lead to the person avoiding situations.

The belief that perfection is possible – and is the only thing that is worth it – and the belief that a person's worth is determined by achievement, are the two irrational beliefs that feed this kind of thinking.

Catastrophising

You can probably guess the sort of thinking for which this aspect of distorted thinking is responsible. A tendency to exaggerate the consequences of an action, thinking of it as a catastrophic event. Albert Ellis referred to this as *awfulising*. Situations that are perhaps unwelcome or unpleasant are upgraded in a person's mind as being *awful* or *catastrophic*.

You're probably very familiar with this, either from times when you've engaged in this kind of thought process or observed others doing it. Highly anxious or stressed people are prime candidates for this mode of thinking. A highly active imagination tinged with 'clairvoyancy' – showing a negative/pessimistic scenario – results in a belief that disaster is inevitable. A lot of 'what if' and 'it's inevitable' type statements become a habit of thinking and in some cases self-fulfilling prophecies.

'It's inevitable that I'll be the first to go when they trim the department. I'll lose the private medical insurance. I'll probably get an injury. The waiting list at the hospital will be horrendous. I won't be able to look for a job . . .'

'What if . . .'

Once again, the end result will be an inappropriate assessment of life or event circumstances resulting in being upset or in distress when the situation doesn't warrant it. You can imagine everyday situations in which you, or people you know and observe, spend time elevating *minor* occurrences to *major* transgressions. The bus being late, the carrots being too hard on a particular day in the staff restaurant, the fact that you accidentally pushed into the queue, a missed dentist's appointment, your son late home from a party. When we're catastrophising with 'should' – style thinking about other people or life in general it often leads to anger: 'He shouldn't keep people waiting that long – it's awful when you've taken the trouble to book an appointment.'

So, we need to keep our thoughts in check and be aware of when we're engaging in this kind of thinking, even when we are encountering major problems. They too can be made more catastrophic than the situation warrants.

Emotional reasoning

This is such a common thinking error that through force of habit you'll probably find that you've been doing this automatically without a moment's thought (literally!).

What happens here is that your feelings dictate what 'reality' is. **Feelings become facts** – as opposed to an emotional state being *experienced*. Something makes you afraid, therefore it has to be dangerous simply because it's something you fear. You feel guilty, therefore you must have done something wrong.

We've been looking at how unhealthy thoughts create our feelings and emotions. But our feelings also contribute to a certain line of thinking, providing *evidence* for a thought. You may experience feelings of awkwardness at a work function you're attending, for example. So you use this emotional response as a catalyst for deciding that this gathering is not for you and you'd rather leave. Obviously, emotions are important for the information they provide, but they have to be interpreted in an objective way to understand what they mean.

Mind-reading

Of course it's our own thinking that causes us problems in life, but there is a form of distorted thinking that we all engage in relating to other people – mind-reading. In our own cases we're inclined to engage in a bit of *telepathy*.

Knowing what other people are thinking is fine for a stage show – if you can pull it off (and I've had my share of successes and failure in that!) – but in real life it's a case of us jumping to conclusions. What conclusions, typically? Well, that people are forming *negative* conclusions about us. There we go again! Isn't it part of the human condition that we always fear the worst? Paranoia sets in and all sorts of imaginative scenarios are played out in the mind. When a person's self-esteem is not that high they tend to engage a lot in this kind of thought pattern:

- 'He snubbed me in the supermarket.'
- 'She deliberately chose to not return my call.'
- 'He thinks I'm unattractive; my ears are too big, that's why.'
- 'I can tell she thought I was too flirty for the job – she felt threatened.'

'True' reasons for the above (think of some of your own as a little exercise in alternative thinking):

- He never saw her in the check-out queue in the supermarket.
- She couldn't hear the number clearly on the voicemail (muffled).
- 'Nice woman – if only I wasn't married.'
- 'She'd be ideal for the job – shame Paul's decided to recruit internally now.'

You take your own negative opinions about yourself (which you define as *facts*) and you believe that others are in agreement with you. All of it deduced by telepathy!

Fortune-telling

Another favourite with which I'm sure you're very familiar. You *know* how something's going to turn out. So you don't put yourself in the situation. **So it becomes a self-fulfilling prophecy.** This is why so many of us hold ourselves back in life.

- 'I won't go to that networking event – there's never anybody interesting there.'
- 'There's no point booking that outdoor concert in the park next month. It'll probably rain.'
- 'It's pointless going for that loan – they'll want to know that I've run a business before, I bet.'

So predictions turn into *facts*. A possibility is turned into a *probability*. Question whether you actually have facts to back up the probability!

It's emotionally draining when we chastise ourselves for the failures we naturally endure in life, as well as the plentiful output of mistakes and errors of judgement. Then there are the regrets of not being confident or assertive in a situation and for being anxious or depressed at certain times. All this kind of self-criticism does is:

- make you experience feelings of frustration, anger, guilt, shame, resentment;
- deny you the opportunity of regarding yourself as a 'whole' person who, like other people, has a share of weaknesses and flaws;
- encourage you to engage in more procrastination;
- discourage you from looking at aspects of yourself that you would like to change;
- further endorse your own low self-esteem.

Sliding doors

We spend a lot of time with this type of thinking, devising alternative realities of what *'could have'* been had this not happened, or had we *'done this instead'*, or *'if only I had/hadn't'* or *'what if'*. There's an interesting, poignant and thought-provoking film called *Sliding Doors* in which the plot revolves around a woman (Gwyneth Paltrow) as she experiences two parallel universes, based on two separate paths that her life could take, depending on whether she catches the London Underground train.

After being fired from her job in the morning, she goes to the station to catch her train home.

It's a clever premise where in the first timeline she catches the train. She gets back to her flat and discovers her boyfriend has been cheating on her. She leaves him. In the second 'reality' she misses the train as the sliding doors close in front of her and decides to find another way home – but not before a mugging and a trip to the hospital does she finally get there. Consequently she's not aware of her boyfriend's infidelity.

The storyline shows how your path in life can hinge on one small, almost insignificant, event – and the 'ripple effect' that spreads out from that. In the two different 'realities' it

Sliding Doors (Gwyneth Paltrow experiences a new 'reality')

illustrates just how missing that train impacted on the character's future in a completely different way than if she had caught it. Needless to say, relationships form the biggest impact in both scenarios.

I won't give the rest of the plot away in case you choose to see it, but the intriguing plotline explores what most of us have said to ourselves – and also berated ourselves about – along the lines of 'if only I hadn't done . . . my whole life could have been so different . . .'.

I find that the most heart-rending message of the plot relates to how we 'beat ourselves up' and 'put ourselves down' in life by inducing anxiety, guilt and negative thoughts as we say to ourselves, 'I should have done . . . and it would have led to . . .'.

As discussed earlier, when we say to ourselves that taking path B – instead of path A which we chose – would have been better because it would have led to 'this' instead of 'that', we're creating a reality that is entirely of our own fabrication.

An example – this is typical of the way that we engage in *clairvoyancy* and make ourselves feel bad at the same time:

Sarah: 'I shouldn't have gone into architecture. The housing market's been so volatile these last few years. Bad decision. I should have been an international corporate lawyer – I could have specialised in foreign mergers and acquisitions – I could have travelled the world – by the time I was 40 I could probably have had a country mansion and a town pad – at 50 I could have retired early and taken an early pension – my husband and I would have been able to have long holidays – the kids would have been finishing university – I'd have lots of free time for grandchildren.'

Okay – excuse me for a moment. **'Sliding doors'**. New reality:

● Sarah didn't take architecture.

● She went for law and passed exams and ended up working for a firm and specialised in corporate law.

● She met someone during her studies and they got married while she was studying.

● She had her first child in the second year of employment at the law firm.

● This put tremendous strain on her as she juggled both areas of life.

● In the meantime her husband was travelling a lot with his job and so with him being absent a lot of the time, she had even more to cope with.

● Not long after – they separated. With a failed marriage, her confidence was knocked; also her son was now experiencing emotional difficulties and the school alerted her to this.

● Instead of relying on child-minders she decided she had to spend more time with him.

● Her work was suffering and she was passed over for promotion twice.

● In addition, she had to have time off for illness as her exhaustion was taking its toll.

● No longer able to cope with her ill-health and her son's problems her performance at work got steadily worse as the workload piled up.

● When the company was taken over by a US 'giant', redundancies were imminent.

● At the age of 32 Sarah received the letter 'finishing' her law career.

What happened to the predictions about how life would turn out based on *'I should have been a corporate lawyer and I could have . . .?'* Where is the country mansion? The early retirement?

Doesn't that just show how we unnecessarily waste time in life with past anxieties of what would have happened if we'd have taken another path? Of course we can learn things so that we make better decisions based on past experiences. But to chastise ourselves and cause mental turmoil based on what we say would have happened – something that we have no control over – is self-defeating.

Laws of nature?

It's not beyond human beings to believe that there are things that happen in the universe – or our own reality – because that's what the laws of nature decreed at *that* moment in time. The universe decides that volcanic ash will disrupt flights and cause havoc to travellers in 2010 – because *that's how it is*. A career decision we make results in eventual redundancy – because *that's how it is*.

We make decisions based on our mind-set and circumstances at a particular time. If at the time our thinking *had* been different and the circumstances had equally been different we may not have gone down a particular path. With knowledge of the past, in retrospect of course we can say we should not have done something and done something else. All we can do is utilise past experience and try to make better decisions in the future. But even those new decisions will be based on our mind-set (albeit better informed) and prevailing circumstances at that time.

So in the example above, Sarah made a decision to be an architect, based on her thought processes and the circumstances at the time. The laws of nature decreed that the housing market would be volatile. She feels dissatisfied at the way things are and criticises herself for making the wrong choice of career. She should have been an international corporate lawyer, she reasons, which would have led to wealth, a country home, long holidays, grandchildren, a big pension . . . by the time she was 50.

What was the true reality? Something completely different.

So the next time your critical self-talk sets out to ruin your life even more, with a prophecy of what would have happened if you'd done something else – taken a different path – just say to yourself in your mind, 'sliding doors'. It will remind you that you do yourself no favours when you indulge in this type of thinking. You can't know exactly what will happen to you in life if you take another path.

Your inner critic

We have to remember that there are two ways of looking at your mistakes and quite often, when caught up in the emotional maelstrom of negative thought, people lose sight of the difference. You can be:

● critical *of* your mistakes;
● criticise *yourself* for the mistakes.

There's quite a difference here. If you're critical of the way you handled something or any other mistaken action then it can be productive as you learn from the situation. The important thing is that the emphasis is on the mistake and not *you* as a person. In theory, you're able to do things differently in similar circumstances another time. By not being too critical and brutal with yourself you avoid expending your emotional energy.

Conversely, when you criticise yourself the focus becomes *you* and not the mistake. You'll know from your own experiences and encounters with other people that this leads to bad feelings and makes it difficult to adopt a more helpful thinking style. It discourages clear thinking and decision-making on how to change things. It leads to that spiral of negative thoughts and behaviour and drains energy and commitment for learning and preventing future mistakes.

People perceiving themselves as a failure (labelling, as we saw earlier) for having made a mistake and for failing – or for not having handled something well – become reluctant to take chances in the future. Our mind is both our greatest asset and our greatest foe when it comes to fearful situations.

Yet success is often only forthcoming after episodes of failure. This fear of failure combined with procrastination leads to achievements being curtailed by unhealthy thinking. As mentioned earlier, if a person is already suffering from low self-esteem and is also overly concerned about what others think of them, this fear of failure is maintained. Remember the story of Thomas Edison and his 700 attempts with the electric light bulb. When asked how it felt to have failed 700 times, he replied: '*I have not failed 700 times. I have not failed once. I have succeeded in proving that those 700 ways will not work. When I have eliminated all the ways that will not work, I will find the way that will work.*' Quite a healthy attitude that we can all learn from and a good illustration of perspective. One view would be critical of the self; the other looks at failure as a pathway to eventual success.

When we challenge or 'dispute' our thinking (which you'll be learning about in the next chapter) and convince ourselves that there is no evidence for feeling this way, we can see that procrastination supports this fear of failure. This challenge helps to create a feeling of confidence and inspires the motivation that is needed to tackle the procrastination.

Remember: we experience things not going the way we would like them to every day of our lives. How we perceive the outcome is an individual thing and depends on our own 'reality'. So how should we regard a failure? It's a *perception* and a *belief*. It's not an *outcome* and a *fact*.

You can see from the different thinking styles we've looked at that we all have various distorted thinking errors to justify our lack of belief in ourselves. The common ones such as perfectionism, black and white thinking, overgeneralisation, mental filters and 'shoulds' will probably be very familiar to you in your thought history. The important point to note is that despite what you have felt previously, **self-criticism does little to steer you in the direction of being productive or positive.** You end up feeling worse about a situation and you use up precious energy that would be better served in helping you to change. As long as we learn something from the experiences, and through renewed thinking minimise these actions in the future, we're making progress.

Tricks of the mind

Let's take some questions from my 'Top 20' that you can ask yourself to challenge your distorted thinking in any situation. You'll find that you'll quite naturally be able to add your *own* questions to this list for specific '**thought attacks**' that you experience.

1   Am I basing this on **opinions** or facts?

2   Am I stuck in this thought-mode through **laziness** in thinking?

3   Is there really any **connection** between what happened in the past and now?

4   Is there a possibility I could be **wrong**?

5   How can I be **sure** about that?

6   What **assumptions** am I making?

7   Are there **examples** to back up my way of thinking?

8   If so, are they **relevant** in this situation?

9   Is this **way** of thinking holding me back?

10   What's the **worst** that could happen?

11   Could I **cope** with that 'worst' outcome?

12   What would [**friend/relative/work colleague**] think of my view?

13 What might they say to me that **refutes** it?

14 Who says things **should** be this way?

15 What leads me to **believe** that?

16 Where's the **proof** of this?

17 Is there another way of **looking** at the situation?

18 Am I taking the blame for something that's not **my** fault?

19 What did I **think** to make me feel better when I had **similar** thoughts?

20 Am I just **jumping to conclusions**?

A lot of scientific research has been done to identify thinking distortions that are common to most people. These patterns of irrational thinking were probably very familiar to you as you read them, even though you didn't realise that one or more of them is a favoured habit of yours.

The key to changing your thinking – and therefore changing your life – is to identify which of these habitual ways of thinking are part of your mental repertoire. It's one or more of these that are holding you back from achieving a lot more fulfilment. Whichever of these faulty thinking angles you focus on, you end up feeling bad. Having identified them you can work on eliminating them gradually.

These thinking habits represent the core causes of self-defeating behaviour. An awareness of which style of thinking you may be adopting will pay huge dividends. As you'll see, it is the beliefs that you hold about:

● yourself;

● the world;

● other people;

that lead to an irrational and negative style of thinking, unhelpful emotions and at the same time prevent you from feeling good about yourself and situations. As always, the key is to challenge these beliefs with your rational self-talk and change your thinking.

I'd just like to share with you an extract from a poem by Walter Wintle:

The Victor

If you think you are beaten, you are,
If you think you dare not, you don't.
If you'd like to win, but think you can't,
It's almost certain you won't.

If you think you will lose, you've lost,
For out of the world we find,
Success begins with a fellow's will,
It's all in the state of mind.

Full many a race is lost,
Ere ever a step is run.
And many a coward fails,
Ere ever his work's begun.

Think big and your deeds will grow,
Think small and you'll fall behind,
Think that you can, and you will,
It's all in the state of mind.

If you think you are outclassed, you are,
You've got to think high to rise,
You've got to be sure of yourself before
You can ever win a prize.

Life's battles don't always go
To the stronger or faster man.
But soon or late the man who wins,
Is the man who thinks he can.

Next we'll be looking at controlling your mind and how you can change your thinking and therefore your life – for the better.

Coffee break . . .

 For most people it's not easy to recognise unhealthy negative thinking patterns as they have often become lifelong habits.

 The assumption is that even thinking that veers towards the negative is still rational. This may be so when your mind is healthy – but in a dysfunctional state of mind this may be irrational.

 Most thoughts are those about an *original* thought – and the cycle continues.

 When you spend your life thinking in a 'distorted' way, you strengthen the connections between the neurons. Result? You become an expert in distorted thinking.

 Negative/distorted thoughts zoom into the mind, do the damage and then flit off again quickly, so you hardly notice what's happened (only the feelings that have been generated).

 Devising alternative 'realities' of what *'could have'* been or what you or someone *'should have'* done, is a path to misery and anxiety. This 'fortune-telling' creates a reality that is entirely of your own fabrication.

 The key to changing your thinking – and therefore your life – is to identify which of the ways of habitual thinking (one or more) is holding you back from achieving more fulfilment.

 You can be *critical* of your mistakes or you can *criticise* yourself for mistakes. The first attitude can be productive as you can learn from the situation. With the second attitude the focus becomes *you* and not the mistake; this makes it difficult to adopt a more helpful thinking style.

Chapter

3

'Man is disturbed not by things,
but by the views he takes of them.'

Epictetus (AD 55 – 135)

Mind control

As you saw in the last chapter, a lot of scientific research has been done to identify thinking distortions that are common to most people.

To reiterate: the key to changing your thinking is to identify which of these habitual ways of thinking are part of your mental repertoire. Having identified them you can work on eliminating them gradually.

It's probably clear to you by now that the premise of this book is this:

> **It is our own cognitions that will decide how we feel and ultimately behave.**

With all of life's 'flotsam and jetsam', the one thing that is within our control to change is our thinking. If we can respond to complications and problems – whether real or perceived – in a non-negative way, it will change our feelings about *ourselves*, other *people* and the *world*.

- The power of our thoughts and beliefs to hold us *back* is colossal.
- Equally, that same mind power has the capacity to propel us *forward* – to achieve more of what we want in life.

Think of it this way. You've seen in the earlier chapters how our mind/brain is an electromagnetic system. Our thoughts are energy. As you focus on a particular thought you are literally taking this energy from your *inner* world and creating something in the *outer* world of reality – based entirely on your thoughts.

That energy resulted in this book you are reading now, that train seat you're sitting on, those spectacle frames on your nose, those nice shoes on your feet, the good cut of your jacket. Your thoughts are the ideas that generate an image in your mind and the energy produced attempts to make it happen.

If only life were that simple. That our minds were following that path of self-belief on a quest for creating positive realities. The truth is this – **for much of the time our minds are hell-bent on sabotaging the path to personal happiness and success**. So much so that we won't have the luxury of experiencing what might be called – if I can invent a term – a 'positive spiral'. But we'll certainly be acquainted with going down that never-ending journey of a downward 'negative spiral' – something with which we're all familiar.

(That's why the next part of this book is concerned with taming that 'tortured' mind so that we can learn how to control that thought energy from negative to a more positive frame – and steer it towards a path of happiness and contentment. Not an easy task, but achievable. We do it through *mind control* – control of thoughts and feelings.)

Unhelpful thinking

We've all been exercising certain thinking habits for many years and like most habits we can't get rid of them overnight. Perhaps the most difficult one of all is the natural human propensity to think in a negative way. Research has shown that most of our thinking comes under the category of 'negative'. A thought occurs and you're on your way down – it happens almost instantaneously. Shocked? See if you can be aware in the next day or so of the content of your thoughts. I think you'll find that it's right.

Take your everyday situations. Let's start off with, say, your breakfast in the morning, your walk to the train station or bus stop or your drive in the car. Then, while you're having lunch, your journey home from work, while you're watching TV and maybe while you're lying in bed. Now, truthfully, evaluate most of the thinking that occurred during the sum total of all these everyday situations. Wasn't it predominantly unhelpful and negative thinking?

Can you now see why it's so important that we tackle this lifelong habit before there's any hope of a changed and more satisfying life? It can be done but there's a lot of undoing to do. The point is that we're never going to be able to stop all negative thoughts. That would be impossible and undesirable. We need to be a little critical – about ourselves, for example – in order for us to be motivated to be better.

It's the *excessive* amount of negative and unhelpful thinking that is the problem. Having the awareness of when it's happening to you and being able to 'flick the switch' and challenge unhelpful thinking (as we'll see with *MindControl*) when it occurs, is the key to a more productive life. Your thoughts and therefore your attitude and, of course, most importantly, the way you feel – all will be transformed.

You may be confused as to which thoughts come under that category. Put simply, when you have some thoughts that make you feel bad about yourself – compared to how you felt *before* you started that thinking process – you can consider that to be just one of your many episodes of negative thinking.

As we discussed in the last chapter, it is when you dwell on certain unhelpful thoughts that the damage occurs. Of course there are some thoughts that cause you genuine problems in everyday life. And these are added to by the day. One gets sorted out – *or never materialised in the first place* – and another two come along. If you can learn to change your habit of giving energy to these thoughts and not allowing them to gather pace, that's the first step.

So we know that we're all guilty of negative thinking and yet we allow ourselves to be controlled by the mind when the reverse should happen.

It's worth restating what we discussed in the first chapter.

When:

- we change our **thinking**;
- we change our **feelings**;
- then we change our **actions**;
- this changes our **life**.

In short, to repeat what we touched upon earlier – your distorted thoughts can only lead to unhealthy, negative emotions. Adopting a thinking style that is more positive and more realistic leads to a change in the way you feel. The important thing to remember is that just as the mind is capable of changing our perceptions of current situations, *it can also work on things relating to the past.*

These past situations can be mistakes you feel you have made in times gone by or perhaps some anger that you're holding onto, from years ago. Bear in mind that whenever we're recalling our past experiences, it's as well to remember that at that specific time we handled things the way we did based on our own mental limitations at the time. We were who we were – at that time. Our thinking process operated in a certain way – based on our knowledge of the world and how we felt about ourselves.

Our actions result directly from our thoughts. If you focus your mind on limitations, that's the path you will go down. 'I'll never be able to do that . . .', 'It'll take ages to see a return on that . . .', 'I can't spare the time for . . .' These self-defeating or self-sabotaging beliefs serve to reinforce our reasons for inaction.

With a bit of reflection you can probably analyse your own patterns of thinking in various situations. What makes you stressed? How much of this could be avoided? Which element requires a change of mind-set that would make you feel better? How could you change a particular behaviour that would in turn change the way you feel?

I'd just like to go back to the first part of that 'earth-shattering' idea that so influenced me as a child (as discussed in the last chapter):

'Whether you're an optimist or a pessimist may not affect the outcome. It's just that the optimist has a better time in life.'

The next stage of my 'eureka' moment was many years later. In the course of my studies in cognitive psychology I was introduced to the work of the American clinical psychologist Albert Ellis, who was the leading light in the 'cognitive revolution' discussed earlier. He formulated the hugely influential cognitive model of therapy known as REBT (Rational Emotive Behaviour Therapy).

So. Whether you're an optimist or a pessimist (drawing on the earlier quote) – it now seemed (in some instances) that it may **affect the outcome**.

You'll see how in the following pages.

How gratifying it was for me to actually come across this new 'therapy' that confirmed what I had found out in my own experiences; that it was a better state of 'being' to adopt. And I noticed that in many cases it *did* affect the outcome – in good ways – as it encouraged you to put yourself into situations which increased your chances of getting what you wanted; allowing a bit of *serendipity* to rear its head now and again. Here was the thought–feeling–behaviour link in action.

What was the thinking behind Dr Ellis's therapy? Well . . . *thinking*, come to think of it!

The art of thinking more philosophically. Ellis was drawn especially to the writings of the Stoic philosophers like Epictetus whose pithiest and most powerful comment was: 'Men are disturbed not by things, but the view they take of them.'

This groundbreaking REBT treatment was based on Ellis's conviction – heavily influenced by the ancient philosophers – that it is:

- our own **thoughts** and **beliefs** that cause our psychological problems;
- these two things determine how we **interpret** the world we live in and how we **feel** from day to day.

Faulty, unhelpful or irrational thinking makes us feel bad, was his rationale. These errors in thinking tend to:

- distort 'reality';
- invite the wrong conclusions; and
- focus on an unfavourable outcome.

Ellis researched and interviewed patients intensively and noted the recurring tendency of humans to interpret events in an irrational way. So, he concluded, our *irrational* thinking was the cause of much of our stress and *dis*tress.

Put simply, if we don't feel good about ourselves or we behave in an irrational manner it is because of our **internal dialogue**.

So influential was Ellis's work that to this day it is widely used all over the world. His idea was that 'thinking errors' and consequently unhelpful processing are the cause of most of our disturbances in life, so the solution lay in challenging and re-evaluating these unhelpful cognitions (thoughts).

In the 1970s and 1980s *present* thinking, as opposed to delving too much into the *past* – the crux of other psychotherapeutic methods – was in favour. The field of psychoanalysis as advanced by Freud became increasingly discredited and the cognitive approach favoured by Ellis rose to prominence. In talking about neurosis – the central concept in the Freudian model

There is no such thing as reality, only perception (you create your own reality through your perception) of personality – Ellis dismissed it as *'just a high-class word for whining'*.

Short-term treatment aimed at changing our way of thinking in the **here and now**, rather than seeking to understand the past, was the tenet of his treatment, with *beliefs* being at the core of this psychological model:

'As I see it, psychoanalysis gives clients a cop-out. They don't have to change their ways or their philosophies; they get to talk about themselves for ten years, blaming their parents and waiting for magic bullets.'

In 1982 a poll of psychologists carried out by the American Psychological Association (APA) voted Ellis the second most influential psychologist of the 20th century – ahead of Freud (and behind Carl Rogers).

Our irrational beliefs

The theory that events in our lives are not the *cause* of our upset, but our *reactions* – based on our beliefs – is the cornerstone of the powerful model that Dr Ellis formulated. It was (behind his strong language) an insightful and forgiving approach to human emotional life, based on the premise that:

- we have negative emotional reactions not to *events* themselves;
- but to our irrational *beliefs* about the events.

Furthermore, we demand that 'reality' should be different to what it is. There are three 'musts' that hold us back (see below), he wrote: *'I must do well. You must treat me well. And the world must be easy.'*

On the basis that all of us have a shared vision in life, namely to be happy, it's a shame that fortune doesn't always agree with us. Our wants, needs and goals are constantly being blocked. We can respond:

- in a manner that is *healthy* and *helpful*; or
- in ways that are the *opposite* and *self-defeating* – unhealthy and unhelpful.

All human beings are different of course, but there are three major and universal irrational beliefs – with different manifestations – that upset everybody and that Ellis called 'The Three Basic Musts'. These relate to:

1 A demand about *ourselves*: I must do well and I have to win the approval of other people or I have failed (leads to anxiety, guilt, depression).

2 A demand about other *people*: People must treat me in a way that I would like to be treated – fairly, considerately and with kindness. If they don't do that it means they're no good and should be condemned for it, and also punished (leads to anger, passive–aggression, violence).

3 A demand about the *world*: I must have what I want, when I want it and I must not get what I don't want. It's terrible if I am unable to get what I want and when that happens, I can't stand it (leads to procrastination, 'victim mentality' and self-pity).

The idea is that because of the inflexible nature of these demands there will always be a problem with unhealthy cognitions. Only by changing the mind-set and adopting more flexible beliefs can healthy emotions and corresponding behaviours occur.

What's the antidote to these major irrational ways of thinking? **Acceptance**.

Acceptance of 'reality' – no matter how unpleasant it seems. So, referring to the three elements above, relating to yourself, other people and life in general, the premise is that we practise three types of acceptance. Each of these is underpinned by three core beliefs.

1 We practise unconditional *self-acceptance*.
   – Accept the fact that you are a fallible person who has both good and bad points like everyone else.
   – There's no reason why you shouldn't have flaws of some sort.
   – You are no less worthy and no more worthy than anybody else, despite your good and bad points.

2 We practise unconditional *other-acceptance*.
   – Accept that other people will inevitably treat you unfairly on occasions.
   – There is no reason why they must treat you with fairness.
   – The people that do treat you unfairly are no more worthy and no less worthy than other people.

3 We practise unconditional *life-acceptance*.
   – Accept that life doesn't unfold the way you'd always like it to.
   – There's no reason why life should turn out the way you want it to.
   – Life may not be what you regard as pleasant but it is not awful and in most instances it is certainly bearable.

The idea that there was now a form of therapy that could target thought processes and also show the link between consequent *emotional*, *physiological* and *behavioural* states caused quite a stir. In the 1960s, taking the foundation of Ellis's approach, the psychiatrist Aaron Beck developed a cognitive therapy for use with patients suffering from depression. Later – with behavioural elements added – it became the now well-known CBT. Beck's treatment differed from Ellis's inasmuch as it focused on a more *clinical* approach. Fifty years later it has now been accepted that:

● we can **choose** the way we think;

● our feelings follow our **thoughts**;

● it's only lifelong **habits** that make us focus and dwell on certain thoughts (mainly negative).

'Present' thinking

The core of REBT and subsequent therapies is an emphasis on the role of thoughts and beliefs in the *present*. The earlier work of Sigmund Freud with an emphasis on the *past* – early childhood experiences – was rejected in favour of changing people's perceptions and their behaviours in what we might call 'the present moment'.

Sounds like a more satisfying approach. After all – life is a *series* of present moments. This approach demonstrates that strong negative feelings such as anger, anxiety, depression or guilt are not fixed by delving deeply into the past life with a full and lengthy biographical journey. These feelings are, after all, generated *moment by moment*, and *situation by situation*, based on a person's attitudes and irrational beliefs about a particular situation. That's not to say that your past life is unimportant. It provides clues as to why you may have adopted various beliefs. These beliefs tend to fall in three main categories which you'll readily understand. Beliefs relating to:

- yourself;
- other people;
- the world.

The aim is to change any inappropriate beliefs that result in unhealthy thinking in your *present* life, in these three main areas, so that you can change it for the better.

1 **By thinking in a more rational (less critical/less negative) manner we change how we *feel*.**

2 **This in turn leads to a change in our *behaviour*.**

Ellis's hard-hitting approach struck a chord with his peers and patients (and later on with students of REBT like myself). It was exemplified by his typical no-nonsense statements, a lot of them delivered at his – standing-room only – Friday lectures in

New York City that ran from mid-1960 to 2007. It doesn't get more direct than this:

'If you're pretty crazy you're in good company, because the human race as a whole is out of its goddam head . . . If the Martians ever find out how we human beings think, they'll kill themselves laughing.'

Seduced by our own thoughts

The idea that thinking in a different way to change your viewpoint makes you feel differently, and therefore leads to you behaving in a different way, is now a big success story.

The premise that power lies with you – the *originator* of the thoughts – rather than with the *actual* thoughts themselves, is key to you changing your life. Otherwise it means you are seduced by your own thoughts.

How much of your failure is due to unrealistic expectations? What is the cascade of cognitions, self-talk and underlying irrational beliefs doing to your self-esteem?

Let's face it – we spend most of our lives succumbing to this seduction, don't we? Don't you spend an awful lot of life's precious time thinking thoughts that arouse strong emotions in you; thoughts that are actually not true and are consequently leading you to devote time, energy and emotion to the wrong avenue? Just because you have a strong belief about something it doesn't mean it's true.

Also, consider this. Do you spend most of your life formulating *positive* and *helpful* judgements about things, events, and other people? Or is it usually the flip side – negative formulations? I know when I ask people in groups to answer with a show of hands, it's about 90% of the people in attendance who admit to negative formulations. Then, after a bit of prompting and questioning, it goes up to the magic 100% – everybody!

Whether you're an optimist or a pessimist may not affect the outcome. It's just that the optimist has a better time in life

Yet the key to healthier thinking is there but for the 'flick of a switch' in your mind. I'm not advocating 'positive' thoughts as an antidote to life's ills. You may have become bored by hearing the term 'think positively' as it's constantly spouted by well-meaning individuals and well-being articles in magazines and newspapers.

It's impossible to believe of anyone that they are able to go through life, day by day, thinking *only* positive thoughts. When the car insurance renewal drops on your doormat, when the waiter spills the contents of the gravy boat on your new dress, when the power-cut comes during a cold spell, when your boss unfairly criticises you, when you realise you've left your mobile phone on the crowded train; life throwing things at you while you're busy making plans.

So please banish those sceptical thoughts (there's another avenue to consider!) as *Mind Power* is ultimately concerned with you:

- challenging your negative thoughts with *alternative* thoughts;
- looking at things from a **different** angle. It's not just about trying to see things in a more positive light; rather it's about *evaluating* your own self-talk to see whether it is valid and then *disputing* its irrationality, if that's the case.

So, as I say during *MindControl* sessions:

> **'Get rid of the negative thinking and the rest of the thoughts will take care of themselves.'**

Change your thinking, change your life

We looked at the thought–feeling–behaviour spiral in the previous chapter. So, if our thoughts affect our behaviours it means that in essence we prime ourselves with our cognitions to be **motivated** to do things – or **demotivated**.

We could change negative thoughts by being more realistic and more rational in our thinking, in *any* situation. For example:

Scenario 1	
Sarah (thinking):	'Hey. That's that lady I met at the Health and Well-Being seminar last year over in Lausanne – told me to keep in touch when she was leaving the cocktail party. Wonder if there are any vacancies at her place? She won't remember me. Just being polite I reckon . . . heard her say those words to somebody else.'
Result:	Doesn't bother to take the chance of going up to her and introducing herself.
Her unhelpful (negative) thinking:	Won't remember me . . . probably just being polite. . . says that to everyone. Who am I, compared to her? Couldn't stand the embarrassment of her thinking, 'Who are you?'
Change of thinking:	What's the worst that could happen? The woman (Diana) doesn't remember Sarah. She could still ask about vacancies. What's the worst that could happen here? No joy. Might she remember her if they met a third time, by accident? Good chance.

Since we know the worst that could happen is that she doesn't remember Sarah, let's take a look at what a more fruitful outcome could be:

Scenario 2	
Diana does remember Sarah:	
Sarah:	Hello, I'm Sarah. I met you at a seminar over in Lausanne last year. You're Diana, HR Director at Cranford's.

Diana:	That's right. I do remember your face – and my daughter's name is Sarah so I do recall our chat. You'd just left a job after many years if I remember?
Sarah:	That's right. I'm still searching for something inspiring in publicity . . . I suppose your company is still not recruiting?
Diana:	Well, as a matter of fact we've got two people to replace in a couple of months. One's maternity leave – the other's a chap transferring over to Frankfurt. I'll give you a card. Can you call me next week?

In this case we can see how:

- a person's *beliefs* were the cause of her initial thinking;
- this influenced how she *felt* and how she *behaved*.

Our beliefs form the basis of how we perceive ourselves, other people and events. These beliefs affect how we **think–feel–behave**. Just as our thoughts influence how we feel and behave, it is the belief that drives the thoughts.

Thoughts come and go, but beliefs are assumptions that we hold that in turn control our thinking. Therefore when we challenge our beliefs it can lead to more productive and non-negative thinking.

In the example earlier, Sarah's beliefs were that she *should* be recognised by the other woman, otherwise it means she was of no consequence to her and that non-recognition would lead to her (Sarah) feeling embarrassed. First, by adopting an approach of 'What's the worst that could happen?', it puts the correct frame around the situation. Secondly, if she didn't recognise her, it was no reflection on Sarah's status. She probably meets many people at many functions. Thirdly, if there were no vacancies, at least she'd met her twice now and if anything did come up in the future, the memory is strengthened.

Scenario 2 – which happened because of a belief change – resulted in a potentially favourable outcome with Sarah in the frame for a possible job offer or at least an ongoing dialogue.

What's the important point here? **Our thinking creates our feelings and our feelings affect our behaviour**.

Sarah's feelings in Scenario 1: she won't remember me (embarrassment in advance!); 'Who am I?' (feeling of inadequacy); no jobs available (feeling of rejection).

If Sarah holds the beliefs that people should always remember her, that other people are better than her (by virtue of job status) and that something not being available at a certain time is a rejection of her, as a person – her thinking can only be classified as distorted or irrational. So, challenge your beliefs and change your thinking.

By changing her thinking, Sarah changed her behaviour. In the first instance her behaviour was to walk the other way and not approach the HR director.

The second scenario led to completely different behaviour, with Sarah approaching her and having an amicable conversation that may be life-changing for her. Two different thoughts and two different outcomes in her life. Because if you **think** in a certain way, it makes you **feel** a certain way – and causes you to **behave** in a certain way to try and attain your goals. Case closed. Now let's elaborate in more detail as to how you can gradually change your way of looking at things in life.

It's as easy as ABC

If you take most people – and I guess you're one of them – they rarely take time to actually observe their thinking. It's as if the thoughts are there as background, slipping in and out, therefore we have no control over the content and quantity.

Pretty sloppy, when you consider that every part of a person's full and varied life – relationships, housing, finances, work, health – is determined by their thoughts and the actions that result from these cognitions. The secret to fulfilment is learning to control your thoughts.

We know that by modifying our thoughts we can feel happier, as we become ultra-aware of actually *observing* what is causing us to experience a poor mood and then actively *challenging* the irrational/negative thoughts.

The science and philosophy of REBT makes it a very powerful psychological approach to a more successful and healthier way of thinking. Having been subject to extensive scientific testing over decades, it also incorporates the philosophical approach of accepting that every individual has their own set of values and beliefs relating to the world in which they live. Also, people differ in their circumstances and this will influence why they have certain beliefs and attitudes.

The key to the effectiveness of this approach is that whilst acknowledging difficulties, you can still change the way you feel through changing self-defeating and unhelpful ways of thinking. The core principle of this therapeutic approach is the ABC model, based on the following very powerful premise:

- it is not **people** or **events** that make a person feel *good* or *bad* about a situation;
- it is our **thinking** that drives the *feeling* (emotion).

In the **ABC** model:

A represents the activating event or **antecedent** (the 'trigger', so to speak).

B represents your beliefs (your **thoughts** about A).

C represents **consequences** (how you *feel*, the resultant *behaviour*, also *physical* bodily effects).

Almost every time – and I've continually tested this in my *MindControl* workshops – a person's tendency is:

- to put the blame on **A** (the situation/activating event);
- for **C** (consequences).

The central tenet of REBT is that it is **B** that causes **C** (and not A that causes C).

In fact, if you rationalise a situation it is B (beliefs) that is responsible for how we **feel** and subsequently **behave**. Make sense?

Okay – let's go back to Sarah and her initial thoughts:

A (activator/situation): Spots Diana.

B (beliefs): She won't remember me (why should she?); it'll be an awkward encounter and I'll be wasting her time. She meets many people in her job.

C (consequences): Annoyance with herself for dithering, slightly racing heart as she ponders 'Should I?' or 'Should I not?' and then – after all that – decides to walk away from the situation.

I think you can see that everything that happened in C – the emotions, the physical sensations and the subsequent behaviour (walking away) was not *because* of A – it was because of the 'self-talk' or thoughts that occurred in B because of Sarah's beliefs.

> In Scenario 2 the outcome was completely different. Sarah challenged her thinking (B) and potentially *changed her life*.

By challenging her thinking, Sarah *changed* her thinking.

This challenge was referred to as **dispute** (or **D**) in REBT terms. Recognising the thoughts and beliefs that lead to adverse or distorted thinking enables us to dispute them. This is the most important aspect in controlling your thoughts and ultimately feeling better about situations.

To put it another way, it is our cognitions that determine the way that we feel about something. It's not the actions of people or events that happen to us that decide whether we feel good or bad. 'There is nothing good or bad but thinking makes it so' (Shakespeare) remember? Of course they provide the situation that stimulates a reaction. But it's the *reaction* that determines our feelings. In other words – the thinking.

We all have different viewpoints, that is a fundamental part of being human. A lot of our beliefs and opinions are shaped by our experiences from the past. We all have our own different 'realities'. Everything is therefore based on perception. Our perception of a person or event or incident will vary compared to another person's.

So of life we can say: **there is no such thing as reality, only perception**.

When asked about their experience after leaving a nightclub one person may say that the music was unreasonably loud, that it was too crowded and that they were huddled up like cattle. Another may say that the music was great and that they met a lot of interesting people.

MindControl

Drawing heavily on my own experiences and Albert Ellis's work I formulated the *MindControl* approach as a non-clinical self-help model that anyone can use to *change* and *control* their thinking. It's easy to inculcate once you start using it regularly. If you grasped the ABC formula that we looked at earlier, it will be much easier for you to pick up quickly.

Look upon this *MindControl* model as a blueprint for healthy thinking. Most people do find it an easy formula to master and remember on a daily basis and once it firmly becomes an *habitual* way of thinking, it leads to healthier emotions and an improved sense of well-being. To put it more succinctly: your life is never quite the same again. All that changes is a sudden awareness of your old style of thinking and how a new way of looking at things will completely change your feelings.

Let's take a look at:

M – Mental activator

I – Irrational thoughts and beliefs

N – Negative consequences

D – Dispute cognitions

Control your thinking/behaviour.

M represents the **mental 'activator'** that sparks off your cognitive activity.

I signifies the **irrational thinking** governed by your *beliefs*.

N stands for the **negative emotions and behaviour** as a *consequence of* **I**.

D is the process of **disputing** your automatic thoughts for a more *realistic* interpretation.

Control: your thinking and behaviour.

Just to reiterate, the important point is to remember the **thought–feeling link** that we as humans are 'cursed' with! When we think in a different way, we feel in a different way and this determines our mood at any one time. It's important to dispute our unhealthy train of thought and so experience a level of emotion that's more appropriate and less condemning so we don't feel as bad.

Let's take this example:

A friend lends you a DVD of *It's a Wonderful Life* to watch overnight. Very nice of her – except, as always, events unfold as life gets in the way of our well-laid plans!

That same afternoon:

M (mental activator):	You leave it in the coffee bar where you both met that morning and nobody hands it in.
I (irrational thinking):	'How could I be so careless? She'll think I'm really ungrateful. She'll never lend me anything again. She's going to telephone me tomorrow to ask how we enjoyed it. What will I say?'
N (negative consequences):	You feel embarrassed and ashamed and anxious. 'I don't think I'll be able to meet her for coffee mornings anymore' is part of your self-talk.

Now, what if you challenged your irrational thoughts and beliefs and disputed (D) your original thinking? It might go something like this:

D (dispute):	'These things happen. I was carrying a lot of bags in the coffee bar when she handed it to me. I'm sure she's left things behind in her life. She's not going to say she never ever wants to see me again – it's only a DVD. It's unfortunate nobody handed it in. Anyway, good news. The store that I called say that it's been re-released in a colour version – and they've got it in stock.'
CONTROL (your thinking and behaviour):	'Sarah's very understanding. I remember she left her mobile phone in the Ladies once. I'll go and get the DVD from the store now. We'll all still be able to watch it tonight and when she calls in the morning I'll tell her about what happened – and of course tell her that she'll be getting a colour version back which I hope *she'll* enjoy watching!'

It's very important to monitor and identify the cognitions that make us feel bad. Only then can we dispute those thoughts. When we do this, the emotions that may otherwise flood our system, leading to a spiral of even more negative and unhelpful thoughts and emotions, can be replaced. With what? With emotions that are more appropriate to the situation.

Replacing feelings and therefore emotions with more realistic and appropriate ones is the aim of disputing (D) and as such is the key to changing and therefore controlling your thinking.

It's all *IN* the m*in*d

In the example above, let's just look at the two different paths of thinking and feeling – *I N and D*.

M:	Loses DVD.
I:	'How could I be so careless?' 'She'll think badly of me.'
N:	Embarrassed, ashamed, anxious. Considers not attending coffee mornings any more.

Only when D is exercised do we gain some *perspective* on the situation and we are able to *change* and control our thinking:

D:	'It happens to other people. Also, at least it's something that can be replaced. Good job I called the store. They've got it in stock and I'll go and get it now. That'll teach me to be more careful. Although, in my defence – I was carrying a lot of bags and I must have put it down on the table while I was searching for the car keys, after Sarah left.'
CONTROL:	'When Sarah calls tomorrow I'll tell her she'll be getting an even better version of the DVD – in colour. She'll understand. I remember her telling me she left her mobile phone in the Ladies last year in Macy's over in New York.'

Just as we saw earlier in the ABC model where B caused C, equally in this model it's not the mental 'activator' (M) – the event – that caused the problem, **it's the I responsible for the N**. It's all *in* the **mind** – that's a handy way for you to remember the two elements in the heat of the moment when you notice the negative thinking and behaviour (**N**) arising from your irrational beliefs (**I**).

Notice how the negative emotions have now been changed through a different way of thinking. Whereas before there were traces of anxiety, etc, it's now changed to initial irritation followed by your feeling of joy at being able to give your friend a better version of the film that you'd borrowed. Also, that initial thought of changing your behaviour (i.e. not seeing Sarah for coffee mornings in the future) has taken its rightful place – it was just an irrational thought.

We can't get rid of all the adverse emotions that we experience in life. That would be unrealistic. What we can do though is to change our thinking and by so doing respond to situations of discomfort in a more appropriate manner that is more realistic and less upsetting.

People with a strong tendency to personalise will *unnecessarily* spend a lot of their cognitive life embroiled in feelings of hurt and guilt that are often unfounded. And it can fracture relationships.

So challenge your thinking (*MINDControl*). Here's another example. See if it rings true with any situations you've been in.

M (mental activator):	The car runs out of petrol.
I (irrational beliefs and thoughts):	'I should have known – even though it's a new car – how little there was in the tank. It's my fault. Nobody runs out of petrol these days. What will John say – I'm

	supposed to go over those departmental budgets with him today. They'll think I'm a right . . . It's my fault. I could have filled up at that last petrol station . . . There should be more petrol stations like there used to be in the old days . . . I'm worse than pathetic.'
N (negative actions and consequences):	Phones breakdown service while in stressed state. When operative says it will be 'up to two hours' because it's a busy morning with the wet weather, the driver, Tom, explodes: 'I've got meetings this morning. Do you have no sense of urgency, woman?!' he screams. She, in turn, repeats her statement and doesn't try, or go out of her way, to see if there is a breakdown van in the vicinity (which might have resulted in an earlier response to his plight). 'I'm sorry, sir,' she says, while he is still raging at her, 'but I'd be grateful if you could confine the breakdown to your car.'

Tom telephones John while he's in an agitated state, heart racing and still annoyed with the breakdown service. Says he won't be in for a few hours now. John's perfectly okay about it. Tells him not to worry. But Tom's still feeling guilty and berates himself for his irresponsible actions. When he does arrive at work, he's in no state to provide meaningful input to the project – this makes him feel more guilty.

All this self-blame, whilst discounting other reasons that may contribute to a situation, results in excessive guilt and hurt which more often than not exacerbate a particular situation. It's such a common thinking distortion. The secret obviously is to take the focus away from you and consider other reasons or explanations – make it easy on yourself. Let's take a look at the D now, which we'll use to challenge the I.

D (dispute):	'It's a new car. They all vary as to how much is in the tank when the red light goes on. I had nearly two gallons still left when it first came on red, in my last car. Important thing is – I'm not going to let this happen again. I'll just ask them at the next service to check that the fuel gauge is functioning correctly – under the warranty – just in case.'
CONTROL (thinking and behaviour):	'John won't mind about this. I can reschedule which day we do it. He'll understand about the car. He bought a new car recently – I know he had a lot of problems with it. Now, where's the breakdown number? Bad weather today – bet I'll have a long wait. Never mind – I can catch up with paperwork in the car, while I'm waiting. Ah, here's the number . . .'

By disputing the original thoughts, Tom's feelings and therefore his *emotional* state is quite different when he makes the call to the breakdown service (i.e. may even get a quicker response because of his calm delivery) and when he calls the office. He can work in the car while he's waiting for the van. When Tom arrives at work he's not in an agitated state. He was able to control his thoughts and so change the way he feels. Nothing in this scenario was different except the way that Tom changed his reaction to events. How you think, feel and act, as always, will be related to your perception as opposed to 'reality'.

You can see how quickly we tend to fall into the trap of unhelpful thinking. When our mind is in a 'tortured' state we can succumb to these irrational thoughts even more. In Part 2 we'll look at this in greater depth.

Coffee break . . .

 The only thing within our control to change is our thinking. Responding to situations – 'real' or 'perceived' – in a less self-defeating way, changes our feelings.

 Your thoughts are energy. You focus on a single thought and take it from your inner world and create something in the outer world of 'reality' – all of this based on your thoughts.

 Research constantly shows that most of a person's thinking is of a negative nature.

 We're never going to stop all negative thoughts; that would be impossible and undesirable. The idea is to first raise awareness and then reduce the excessive amount of unhelpful thinking that holds you back in life.

 Our own *thoughts* and *beliefs* cause our psychological problems. These two things determine how we *interpret* the world and how we *feel* every day.

 It's not the events in our lives that cause us upset (as Dr. Albert Ellis reminded us) but our reactions to them (based on our beliefs).

 Ellis's form of therapy targeted thought processes, showing the link between emotional, physiological and behavioural states. So successful was his REBT that it spawned the now popular cognitive therapies.

 Pay attention to the cognitions that make you feel bad and then dispute them.

 Exercise mind control using the *MindControl* formula. Remember: I is *responsible* for N (not M). Control your thinking.

The premise that power lies with you – the originator of the thoughts – rather than the actual thoughts themselves, is key to changing your life.

(a) With your *MindControl* you're looking at things from a different angle; it's not just about seeing things in a more positive light. It's evaluating your self-talk and disputing the irrationality.

(b) It's unrealistic to think we can eliminate all negative emotions we experience. But we can change our thinking and, by doing so, respond to discomfort in a more realistic manner.

Part

2

The 'tortured' mind

Chapter

'When I read about the evils of drinking,
I gave up reading.'

Henny Youngman

The stressed mind-set

In this chapter we'll look at the subject of the stressed mind. We'll look at the 'why' of stress and the ways in which it can be 'downgraded' to a more acceptable level that we can term '*pressure*'. Also, in Chapters 5 and 6 we'll focus on the two elements of 'psychological' stress to which we're subject when we face a perceived 'threat' – anxiety, which produces the emotional response of fear and also anger. We experience these different moods alongside our more agreeable states of feeling optimistic, confident and happy.

Knowing how to handle these emotional states is crucial to our well-being.

A stressed mind is out of control. You need to regain control of your life and the world around you.

- Control is seen by stress and anxiety researchers as a fundamental element in relation to the stress situation.

But what *is* this term 'stress' that seems to be bandied around indiscriminately, that we read about constantly and seems to be talked about all the time? A catch-all term that would appear to cover a multitude of sins and is said to affect everyone in varying degrees. Sometimes it's referred to in the sense of what is happening to us in a particular situation: 'It's manic at the moment at work – it's all stress with this new office move.' 'Stressful time at home at the moment – Sue and Matthew have exams coming up.' Other times it's used to describe a physiological feeling that people experience: 'I can't meet up tonight, I feel too stressed.' 'I find this whole airport experience too stressful.'

The stress spiral can cause even more problems when people search for ways to numb their mental state.

They may turn to excessive consumption of alcohol, for example – tempting when you feel the need for a pick-me-up ('Now where's that last bottle of red?'). It provides relief by numbing the brain. At the same time, because it works on the brain in a matter of minutes, it straight away alters the mix of neurochemicals, increasing the release of dopamine and serotonin – providing instant relief. **So 'binge thinking' may lead to 'binge drinking'!**

If not 'self-medicating' with alcohol, during a stressed state, some people use recreational (and prescription) drugs. These drugs trigger a flush of dopamine which increases a sense of feeling relaxed, so they can become highly addictive.

Others will increase their intake of nicotine as they increase their consumption of cigarettes, which again triggers an instant release of dopamine. Some indulge in overeating to deal with their state of mind.

Do you consider yourself to be suffering from stress at this very moment? If your answer is in the affirmative, don't worry – and pile further stress upon yourself – you're in good company.

Surveys in the UK and USA continually show that between more than 50 and 70% of people – at any one time – are extremely concerned about the amount of stress in their lives. Furthermore, a 'Stress in America' survey carried out by the American Psychological Association (APA) in 2007 showed that *job* stress is the number one source of stress for individuals.

Types of 'stressors'

Other results relating to our behaviours during stress in the APA survey were also interesting – although not surprising. One-fifth of drinkers reported drinking too much; two-thirds of smokers said they smoked more; half of the people surveyed said they had disturbed sleep; and nearly one half of the respondents admitted to either overeating or reaching for unhealthy or 'junk' food.

Stress invades our life in a number of categories:

- work stress
- money stress
- parenting stress
- relationships stress.

Then on top of all these we have the everyday: the washing machine's broken down, lost my mobile phone, automated telephone systems ('press one for . . .'), car won't start, forgotten my umbrella-type of stress. So you can see that it comes in a variety of disguises and plans its assault on us from the time we get out of bed.

A stressor can be external – in the sense that it comes from your senses, something you see, hear, feel, taste or touch – or internal, a thought that you hold. What's important to be aware of though is that all stressors end up being internal – in other words, they end up as part of your thought process; and a troubled one at that.

Stress tends to be classified into two areas relating to its severity: minor and major. The minor areas are the everyday ones that we endure (such as those noted above). The major ones are the life events that tend to be more significant: illness, moving house, a new job, a promotion at work, redundancy, divorce, new baby.

It's interesting that when people are asked which of the two stressors are the most disruptive and unhealthiest, most people will say the major ones. Yet all the research – from the consulting rooms, therapist's offices and kitchen tables – shows that it is the small stressors on an everyday basis that 'break the camel's back'.

Because the minor stressors are so relentless and we get used to the assault, we tend not to take them as seriously as the major stressors – which occur less frequently and usually make us focus on getting through the problem.

Perception of stress

What's your idea of stress? Do you find what other people regard as stress – perhaps at work, for example – as simply the pressure you would *expect* to experience in a particular work or life situation? Isn't life, by its very nature, bound to throw up 'stressors' that we need to handle on a day-to-day basis? Doesn't life seem just like a relentless state of emergencies and deadlines to be met? Or is some of it attitude? Are there some things we could handle better by reacting in a different way – by thinking in a different way, in other words? What some people regard as stress others may merely think of as pressure.

Pressure, in many instances, is a positive state of affairs as a certain amount keeps us motivated and challenged whether in a work situation or in other life activities. For some people that very same pressure would be regarded as stress.

In the workplace, for example, pressure can be a motivator and inspire creativity, excitement and a desire to get a job or project done. It's what pushes us towards attaining our goals and our dreams. Stress may occur if pressure becomes too excessive. Loss of control and a feeling of not being able to cope replaces the pursuit of goals. So a positive situation has turned into a negative one.

At this point the natural equilibrium of the body becomes disturbed and if you experience a feeling of being overwhelmed by events then what were previously motivators become looming problems. If the situation continues for too long then we enter that undesirable point of the stress 'spectrum' termed *chronic* stress.

Therein lies the problem in defining stress. What is regarded as a stressful situation varies with different people. As you would imagine, we can't disregard the twin elements of our early life plus genetic predisposition in shaping the way that different individuals respond to what happens to them in life.

How you respond to things that happen to you may be influenced by your personal exposure to stressful situations in your early years, according to continued research.

It was found that some people who had grown up experiencing repeated stress-inducing situations – compared with those who had not – showed more visible stress and increased cortisol production when confronted with mildly stressful situations in later life.

We spoke about perception earlier on. A stressful situation for one person may be thought of in a completely different way by another. The difference? Their perceptions.

As we discussed at length in Chapter 2, you can choose how to react in any particular situation. So the difference between stress and pressure is purely down to the perception of the event.

Therefore we can define stress as a situation in which a person:

perceives **that the demands made upon them exceed their ability to cope**.

We're back to thinking again, as the word 'perceives' indicates. We have to recognise that a person's perception of stress will determine their attitude to a situation. You'll have often witnessed a situation in which another person remains calm or indifferent to a situation that another finds extremely stressful.

Maybe at work, for example, you're told that you've been selected to give a talk on a particular topic at a regional meeting along with a colleague in your section. His interpretation of events:

(thinks):	**'I'm proud they've chosen me. I'll wow them with some figures and graphics – VP from Beijing coming over too.'**
Your interpretation:	**'I don't believe it. I've got enough on at the moment without having to prepare for this – hate speaking at these things. VP's going to be there too. Bad back . . . no, that won't work . . .'**

How common is it these days to hear somebody say to you, 'I'm stressed out'. And how often after comparing your own personal 'brickbats' and 'challenges' have you thought to yourself, 'Well, a lot of that, in my view, sounds like life rather than stress'. If we're experiencing stress our mind is telling us we feel threatened by a 'situation' and, more importantly, our belief is that we are unable to meet the challenges of the threat.

It is our interpretation – or perception – that is the driving force. At times we are right to feel a certain way – the stress and the emotions generated can act as a warning system, enabling us to be aware and take action as it alerts us to a threat.

At other times it is our 'distorted thinking' that may be overly critical, or leading us to form ill-founded conclusions about events or a person's actions. The result – a train of negative thoughts that can lead to unhappiness, an undermining of our self-confidence and a spiral of further stress.

It's important to know what the electrochemical process does to you when you're exposed to a stressor. As we know, there's a certain point when you evaluate a thought and dispute it and either the original 'distorted' or fearful thought remains or you change your thinking – and therefore your feelings. So it loses that control over you.

If it progresses beyond this stage it will pass through two areas of the limbic system – the thalamus and the amygdala. It is the purpose of the thalamus to interpret information coming into the brain and pass it on to the memory network. The memories of your previous emotional responses that the amygdala has stored from similar encounters will produce a knee-jerk emotional response.

Very rarely is stress just one single 'stressor' – it's *cumulative*. It piles up to a point where your mind and body are unable to keep up with the onslaught and that constant 'trickle' of anxiety sets in. Sound familiar?

Yet stress is a natural part of modern life, such is the pace to which we've become accustomed. All the time spent walking on earth is bound to yield different problems from day to day. How we choose to think about these complications – as we discussed in the previous chapter – determines our effectiveness in dealing with them.

Left unchecked, stress grows and follows that downward path as negative interpretations pile onto each other in the mind.

- We'll refer to **stress** as *the reaction to demands made upon us.*
- **Stressors** are *the events, conditions, or circumstances that trigger stress.*

It's important to get this clear at the outset, as there are many definitions out there, even though they all ultimately relate to the same thing. It is worth pointing out the official definition of stress in the UK, as provided by the Health and Safety Executive (HSE):

'The adverse reaction people have to excessive pressures or other types of demand placed on them.'

Notice the term '*excessive* pressures . . .'. Some instances may just be regarded as normal 'pressure' by one person but for somebody else they would fall into the category of stress, with all the related physical and behavioural outcomes. Or one particular event which may be justified as 'pressure' could tip the person over – along with all the other things with which they are dealing – into a stressful state. Be aware that different stressors are ultimately cumulative, so the 'big' life stressors combined with our everyday situations will determine the level of stress that you'll experience.

Again, perception is at the root of our interpretation – as events or situations in themselves are not stressful, in the true sense. A lot may also depend on the 'type' of person – their personality – and their threshold for coping, as well as the coping mechanisms upon which they are able to call.

Are you stressed?

Stress produces a range of signs and symptoms. The following table shows some common ones identified by scientific research as well as the HSE. It's not an exhaustive list of the symptoms but if you feel that your attitude or behaviour is changing due to a situation at work or at home, these may indicate stress. In the table put a tick in the appropriate column of the Stress Audit for the descriptor that you think applies to you. (It's a handy exercise just to remind you of the elements that can lead to a stressful existence – and which we may take for granted, and consequently think is 'normal'.)

Stress audit	Rarely	Quite often	On occasions
Mental • concentration difficulties • money problems • indecision/procrastination • low self-esteem			
Emotional • feelings of anxiety • feeling depressed • feelings of sadness • touchy/irritable • prone to anger • fatigued/drained of energy			
Physical • sleep difficulties • constant tiredness • back/chest/shoulder pain • headaches • depleted immune system			

Behaviour			
• increased drinking or smoking • outbursts of anger • relationship problems • sexual problems • avoiding contact with people • change of eating habits			

When you glance at your sheet of paper, what is it telling you?

Stress can be tackled when people understand how and why it occurs and where there is a real determination to take positive action.

It is important to take action and to review your lifestyle to see if you can identify any factors contributing to stress:

- rushing, hurrying, being available to everyone;
- doing several jobs at once;
- missing breaks when at work, taking work home with you;
- having no time for exercise and relaxation.

Let's look at the typical stress symptoms in terms of the four dimensions that are affected when we reach a certain build-up of pressure that tips us over into what we regard as the stressful state. The four areas are:

1 Mental
2 Emotional
3 Physiological
4 Behavioural.

Situation 1

During a meeting your boss reveals to you and announces to all the others present that you've been chosen to organise the new Cinema Advertising Awards ceremony and given the task of dealing with some Hollywood agents to try and bring over some 'A list' guest presenters.

- *'I'll never handle this'* (**mental**).
- You register feelings of anxiety and fear (**emotional**).
- You experience a rapid heartbeat, dry mouth and your thinking becomes impaired (**physiological**).
- You decide to make your excuses and avoid the situation, thereby jeopardising your chance of being assigned a lucrative project in the future (**behavioural**).

Can you recall the last time you went through the stages described above? What happened? Was it in the same sequence? In other words: this happened – this is what I thought – this is how I felt – and this led me to do *xyz*.

Can you remember at what stage you could use the *MindControl* technique to challenge your thoughts?

In the model above, if a person merely *perceived* the event as 'pressure' rather than stress, then the process, caused by just a change of *thinking*, would be:

Situation 2

- 'Hey, this sounds like it could be fun – I'll give it a go. What's the worst that can happen' (**mental**)?
- Feelings of excitement and apprehension (**emotional**).
- Butterflies in stomach, little bit of shallow breathing at first (**physiological**).

- Gets to work on researching and talking to other people who can help make the project a success (**behavioural**).

So the two different perceptions resulted in the depiction of two different 'realities'. As you know from the last chapter, we can challenge our thinking to prevent the downward trajectory of thought, but the negative or unhelpful thought usually comes into our mind first.

We're all subject to two forms of stress that can be classified as acute and chronic.

Acute stress

This is when we're subject to an immediate situation calling forth our fight/flight response as we're faced with an uncomfortable situation (another 'sardine' experience on the packed London underground train) or challenge (a work interview) or thrilling experience (big dipper ride or acting debut on stage). When the 'threat' is over this type of stress disappears and the body quickly returns to normal.

Chronic stress

This is the more destructive of the two forms as it involves the everyday 'stressors' that we experience on a continual basis. In other words, the long-term exposure to the kind of situations we classify as acute stress that occur in our personal and working lives. With acute stress, the bodily changes eventually return to equilibrium after the 'event' has passed. In this case we're constantly assaulted by the stressors and the body is on a constant state of alert. The alarm never gets switched off. Ongoing people relationship difficulties (in personal/working life) and continual money problems are two areas that contribute to this kind of stress over a long period.

Internal or external?

As you're aware, the stress that you suffer from day to day is not just caused by your reaction to some external event that you've experienced but also by internal reasons. You've already become well acquainted with the 'thinking errors' in which we all indulge as thoughts occur to us. Then our self-talk generates feelings that take on a life of their own. These can result in self-induced stress due to our own attitudes, expectations, fears and insecurities.

These are **internal stressors**.

At other times we're obviously exposed to external events such as major life changes, financial problems, environment problems, work difficulties, relationship difficulties.

These are **external stressors**.

As all human beings are different in the way they perceive things, there will always be situations where what one person regards as stress another would regard as 'pressure'. We all differ in terms of how much pressure we can take, whether it be in a working situation or in life generally.

A certain situation for one person may generate all manner of negative and fearful cognitions which may cause a personality change, eat away at their confidence and may even lead to serious depression. For another person it may just be some added pressure to deal with within a certain time limitation – and it may be the deadline, rather than the task itself (as with our 'stressed out' person) – that is making them experience the pressure.

The important thing to consider is the mind–body connection. Remember this:

There is a **physiological** *difference* between perceived stress and perceived pressure:

- A person enduring stress will exhibit much higher levels of stress hormones coursing through their bloodstream than their counterpart who just feels *pressured* or challenged.

- Every time you encounter a 'perceived' threat your hypothalamus 'presses the buzzer' to set off the alarm and release a surge of the requisite hormones. It then passes a message to the brain centres dealing with fear and your mood state.

- So when your body is in a troubled or tense state the 'pharmacy' in your brain is dispensing a different set of chemicals compared to when you're in a relaxed state – so you *feel* very different and your *thoughts* will be different.

In view of that, we have a good enough reason already to change our mind-set in order to have healthier physiology.

There will also be a *body language* change that should be easy to detect. You know the tell-tale signs of non-verbal language that display tension. Feelings and emotions follow *thought*, and these feelings are 'leaked' through the body.

Performance-wise, most people are at their best when there is just *enough* pressure and they feel stimulated and creative. Pressure for one person is stress for another.

If we experience **not enough** pressure:

- we can become disinterested and bored with situations and jobs.

If we experience **too much** pressure:

- this can lead to stress and anxiety.

Have you ever had to ask for help from a computer technician to solve a software or programing problem for you, asap, and noticed how unruffled and challenged the person was, whilst still aware of the clock (healthy 'pressure')? Quite different from somebody else you dealt with in the past who, faced with your deadline, was sighing, drumming their fingers, swearing (!), and generally getting hot under the collar as their breathing became heavier and heavier (stressed/anxious).

Same request – two *different* reactions, with body language giving away the difference in internal states between the two people.

Stress is a *psychological* and *physical* reaction to life's events. If you reach a stage where you're unable to manage life's vicissitudes, both the mind and body pay a price. Two forces are at play in a person's mind when they feel stressed:

1 There is a sense of threat about the situation(s).

2 The belief is that they will not be able to meet the threat.

The body has a natural alarm system – the oft-quoted fight/flight response. The body and the brain are affected. So we can say that stress acts as a trigger for this response (more about this later).

In order to be free from anxiety/fear and also anger (which we'll cover in the next two chapters) we need to take a look at how stress affects us. Our bodies have been designed to experience the *same* physical reactions when we're in situations that generate pleasure and excitement as they do when we're experiencing an adverse situation.

Don't try to
carpet the world.
Buy a pair
of slippers

Coping with the stress

We all need a little stress to act as a motivator – but when we experience too much it creates an imbalance that throws everything off-course and upsets our equilibrium. The 'spectrum' of stress ranges from what might be termed a state of mild arousal – having to concentrate hard during an important meeting for example – to a situation where you can't think straight and your body is under threat as you experience anxiety and maybe head towards depression.

Obviously, we look to reduce our stress only in situations that are causing us distress. You'll remember from the previous chapter the groundbreaking REBT and my subsequent *MindControl* formula:

> **Thoughts – *produce* – Feelings/Emotions – Behaviour.**

As you now know, thinking is everything. Nothing is more important than that (except breathing). With the stress cycle, everything begins with a person's thoughts.

Just a reminder at this stage:

> **It is the *interpretation* of what happens to you that is important rather than what happens to you.**

Your thoughts are responsible for your emotions which in turn affect your physiology. As you learnt in the previous chapter it is not the situations or events that you are exposed to – or the people that you deal with – that generate your **emotions**. It is the *meaning* that you choose to give to the situations and people. This puts you in a position of control, remember?

Of course sometimes we are perfectly right with regards to our self-talk; we may actually be in the midst of events that are dangerous where we may be physically threatened – or in lesser situations where, equally, the 'threat' produces stress and the accompanying emotions. Here the stress acts as a warning system to prepare us for potential action.

First of all, take an analytical look at the stressors that are causing you problems:

- How many are you *creating*?
- How many are you *maintaining*?

That report you're supposed to hand in – the one that's now nearing the deadline. Is it procrastination that is responsible for the stress rather than the deadline date that is now looming? If that is the case then you haven't taken control of something that was in your control. *Combating stress in certain areas is about taking control.*

We all have a certain point at which the stresses and strains that we're put under lead the body to tell us 'enough is enough'. Yet I'm sure you've come across people who seem to regard the stressed state as something highly desirable. They become addicted to stress. Sounds daft, but these people are serious stress addicts.

They crave the adrenaline rush – the 'high' – as they lurch from one crisis or challenge to another. You've seen this type of person – they create stress out of a situation when it wasn't there before. They are agitated and restless if there isn't much drama going on.

If you're in the company of this type of person it can be debilitating and also contagious. If these are symptoms you recognise in yourself, be aware of the physiological damage they are causing, let alone the relationship problems. Stress addicts are naturally prone to anger and more severe forms of anxiety. Try and recall the last time you didn't have the feeling of being overwhelmed. If you can't – it's time to take stock.

The different types of stressors that we come up with in everyday life – and you're all too aware of most of them – all require different coping techniques.

There are four techniques for dealing with stressful situations identified by psychologists over the years. They are known as the 4 As:

1 ADAPT
2 ACCEPT
3 AVOID
4 ALTER.

They each require change. A change in either:

- your reaction;
- the situation.

Adapt and Accept (involve a change in your **reaction**).

Avoid and Alter (involve a change in the **situation**).

As to which is the most suitable for a particular situation, because *we* are all different and all *situations* are different, too, any one or more of these may prove powerful enough to reappraise the situation. Whichever one improves your mental well-being, giving you a feeling of being able to cope and regaining control, will be the one that is effective.

Let's take a look at the first two – Adapting and Accepting – which both involve a change in your reaction, in other words, your 'thinking' about the situation in order to produce a more productive reaction.

Adapt

The idea is that if you're unable to change the particular stressor then change yourself – in other words, change your thinking. This is something you now understand. If you're able to adapt to the stressor by a change of *attitude* you can put yourself in control again. Life's just not that urgent.

You might say to yourself in certain situations:

- 'While we're stuck in a traffic jam – good opportunity to put on that *French in Three Months* CD.'

- 'I wonder if I should be expending precious energy getting stressed-out and worried over this particular problem – the problem will still be there and I've got to do something about it. Who wants a double whammy – worry and having to sort it out? Not worth it.'

- 'Is this really important to life? Will it mean anything in, say, six months' or a year's time?'

- 'So what if he gets the promotion and I don't. There are always upsides. I won't have to get in at seven o'clock and also I would have had to report to . . .'

Remember the following:

1 Give yourself time to change your thinking and therefore your response.

2 Don't be tempted to react to a situation immediately. Count to ten before speaking, or to free yourself from your unhelpful mental self-talk.

3 When you've calmed down a little you can formulate a more objective response.

Accept

We've got to be realistic and understand that since 'life is not fair' there will always be stressors that we're unable to do anything about. They're simply out of our control. This should always be the first question you ask yourself – is it something within my control? Recognising this at the outset can eliminate an awful lot of heartache down the line.

Remember that most stress is an *internal* response to an *external* event (the M and I, respectively, in our *MindControl* model). So if you can't change the external event (the traffic jam) you have to look to yourself.

If it is internal, set about working out a solution but otherwise, to worry about these situations is to pile on unnecessary layers of negative thought leading to a generalised state of anxiety – which then affects other areas of life.

- We sometimes have to accept that life is the way it is and there are certain things beyond us – which we just don't understand. Acceptance is often the only answer to preserve our well-being.

- Sometimes it helps to bring to mind a situation similar to the one that is causing you discomfort and to try and recall what 'technique' you used as a coping mechanism at the time.

- Other people's behaviour is a constant source of irritation for us. Instead of enduring stress over what, essentially, you can't control (don't you find most people to be stubborn?), train yourself to change your reaction. The one thing that you can control.

- If you have the opportunity, talk to someone you trust about a situation as it can be very cathartic and you may even learn something.

- Each time a stressor comes your way it's helpful to adopt the stop–look–listen approach (see overleaf) which forces you to analyse your automatic stress response. As a threatening situation unfolds and you feel a stress response coming over you, first of all, in order to gain that important element of control, try and minimise your feelings of anger and resentment by 'reframing' your thoughts and letting go of the negative feelings. You get the benefit.

● If you make a poor decision that causes you and others stress, accept that it turned out that way and use the knowledge to try and minimise the risk of further mistakes. Leaving aside wanton and reckless behaviour, we're all learning – all the time.

STOP: suspend your automatic stress thoughts and decide.

LOOK: and observe that you are being exposed to a stress trigger (that's not imminent danger, in the true sense) and decide whether getting upset about the situation will actually change anything.

LISTEN: to your internal thoughts as you alter your perception and accept that nothing useful will be served by resisting a situation (roadworks, post office queue, flight delay, rude and unhelpful receptionist).

Remember that *resistance* paralyses the mind; *acceptance* frees the mind to think more clearly and work on solutions that work for you.

In any case, many of life's activities and irritations are transient – having to act in your daughter's school play (for parents) at Christmas, an upcoming driving test or an exam of some sort, finishing the last chapter of your book before deadline. We can see the end is in sight.

Other events, of course, may be more challenging in their nature, with far-reaching consequences – a house move, illness, new job, separation. We have to accept these adverse situations and work out coping mechanisms that focus on accepting rather than 'curing'.

Try as you might, there are certain things that we all are unable to change. **Don't waste time and energy trying to control**

the uncontrollable. You're probably familiar with the Serenity Prayer which sums it up very well:

> *. . . grant me the serenity*
> *to accept the things I cannot change;*
> *courage to change the things I can;*
> *and the wisdom to know the difference. . .*

The next two techniques – Avoid and Alter – are concerned with changing the **situation**.

Avoid

Sometimes the only way out is to use the avoidance strategy. We can take control of some stress triggers.

Is a lot of your stress due to taking on too much? Is it people's demands? Are you being 'too nice' or 'too empathetic' and suppressing your true thoughts when people pile on more and more requests. Then:

Practise the power of NO.

A lot of people tell me that they are uncomfortable about saying 'no' and that leads them to having 'too much on their plate' at any one time, leading to feelings of being out of control and highly stressed. In order for them to feel better disposed towards exercising their right to use this two-letter word, I ask them to imagine the letters NO as standing for:

Negative

Overload

I ask them to visualise the future and see how the consequence of saying 'yes' now can lead to NO (Negative Overload).

Of course its okay to agree to do things, as we all do, but we're all also guilty of taking on more and more little demands and requests that can add up and lead to overload. Further, it causes us to lose focus on the more important things we should be attending to.

Most people, when asked to reflect on the reason why they are – at any one time – doing things they ideally would not like to be doing, come out with one simple response. They find it difficult to utter the two-letter word. You know how it is; you feel uncomfortable about refusing a request. Sometimes you do it because you want to be helpful in a friendship, family or work situation. At other times you'll do it because it's requested by somebody who has *control* over you – quite often in a work situation.

Perhaps you feel that not taking on that extra task may reflect negatively on you in your working relationship. It may be unfounded, but the fear of what the other person may think prompts you to say 'yes':

'I know he'll think I'm uncooperative – then he'll suggest that I should be first in line for the chop – then we'll only have one income and John will have to work extra hours – he'll be home late . . .'

(A bit of mind-reading, as detailed in Chapter 3, and some 'catastrophising' for good measure.)

So we quite often harbour resentment as our stress levels rise because of the extra tasks we have taken on. We may complete the task and still have antagonistic feelings towards the person who made the request. It's worth listening to your thoughts and feelings before you decide to take something on. When you're asked:

● be in the moment and listen to your instinctive internal response;

● be aware of the feelings that it produces;

● recognise that these emotions are revealing your instinctive thoughts about the situation. If you suppress them – as we tend to do in order to be obliging – they like to come back and 'revisit'.

If your feelings are that you would like to say 'no', then collect your thoughts and come out with the word immediately – and then supply the 'reason' (if you feel you would like, or need, to give one). It sounds more decisive and lessens the chance of the other person trying to get you to change your mind:

'No, I can't at the moment.'

'No – I don't feel I'm able to do this justice because . . .'

'No, I'm under pressure because I'm meeting a deadline for David's quarterly . . .'

'No – I'd gladly help out under other circumstances but with Alison's illness . . .'

It helps if the body language is congruent with your statement so make the tone assured and remember eye contact when you're delivering it. That is, avoid looking at your shoes, the ceiling, the sky, your sandwich, or your BlackBerry.

Eliminate some of the stress in your life by refusing – obviously in the appropriate way – those things that can leave you feeling overwhelmed. As you say 'no', just visualise the words 'Negative Overload' in your mind and eventually you'll find it validates your feelings as you feel less guilt about something that is designed to promote your own well-being.

Avoid a situation or an environment.

I was discussing a situation with a woman who said she got 'stressed-out' as she was constantly fuming in long post office lines to buy stamps – and what made her mad was seeing the staff put the shutters down and close counters at intervals, even though they could see the long queues.

I suggested to her that perhaps she could avoid being in this situation by asking herself if there was an alternative. Maybe she was near certain shops that sell books of stamps – shops that she already uses to buy her public transport travel cards and news-papers. That way she could avoid being in a stressful situation that raised her blood pressure, pushing her to the tip of anger and being mildly rude to the counter staff.

When I met up with this person again a few months later, when she attended another of my workshops, I asked her about her stress levels relating to stamps. She told me that she hadn't set foot in a post office for stamps for months (only to renew her TV licence and car tax on just two occasions – and she made sure it wasn't at lunchtime). She now got her stamps from the newsagents.

As to 'why' she hadn't done this before? She hadn't thought about it, until I had mentioned it to her and, more importantly, it was out of habit. Stamps were associated with the post office. A thinking habit. As we all know – habits are hard to break.

Equally, take a situation where perhaps you've always driven to work or to visit somebody using a particular route and things have changed now – and the level or speed of traffic is causing you stress. Is there a way of avoiding the daily morning scenario that leads you to arriving at work and then spending the first 20 minutes regaling a bored audience with your traffic tales?

Obviously the stressor isn't going to change – *you* have to change. Perhaps by leaving a little early maybe? Or research-ing an alternative route? Using an alternative method of transport? Changing your job, even (if there's scope to do that and it's something that you keep promising yourself you might do 'one day')?

As the saying goes: '*If you do what you've always done, you'll get what you've always got.*'

Avoiding people

Sometimes we just have to make a decision to remove ourselves from situations where we are dealing with people who cause us problems. We interact with people we might regard as 'drains' and 'radiators'. If it gets too much and you're clearly unable to deal with the former – who drain your energy – then try to be in the company of those people who radiate optimism and well-being. You may not be able to permanently extricate yourself from interactions with certain people – in some cases you may – but you may be able to reduce time spent with them.

Alter

We can change the way we handle a stressor by altering the circumstances relating to it to give ourselves more control. Just deal with things in a different way – change the way that you normally operate in your everyday life, whether at home or at work, so that you're not experiencing the same feelings as before.

For example, if you were constantly taking calls directly from staff, because you prided yourself on always 'being available', and you find it interfering with your own work – you're having to stay late – your partner gets angry with you – your children miss out on their 'quality time' with you. This chain of events means you're stressed at work and at home.

It's within your power to control events at work – perhaps using one of the secretaries as a 'screen' who can intercept calls when you're busy and tell staff you'll get back to them. Your 'perfectionism' attitude of 'being available' at all times is still preserved. You're just being sensible about processing the callers' requests to suit your circumstances.

Take another situation, the root of which is time management (the cause of a lot of stress, I'm sure you'll agree). You're constantly being flooded with letters and bills at home and because you feel you can't face dealing with mail shots, financial demands and the rest of the mail, you tend to push them all aside for another time – unopened.

The pile grows by the week. This leads to more procrastination and important items of correspondence are not dealt with. This leads to more stress as you try and 'fire-fight' to make up for your inactivity. This leads to a spiral of stress when added to your work demands.

Alter your time-management a little. Maybe open the envelopes so you at least know what's pressing. Put them in two files and deal with them weekly. You feel on top of the situation when the new batch of mail comes in. Do the same again. You regain some control and consequently control the amount of potential stress that you create.

In your dealings with people, if something is not quite right and is the source of much stress for you, then assertively point out your concerns to try and alter the situation. Failing to do this is the cause of much resentment with families, friends and in the workplace. Nothing changes and so the frustrating situation remains the same and resentment just grows until the 'pressure cooker' can take no more. (You're familiar with what happens next.)

As always, we're dealing with changing habits. When we behave in a certain way for a number of times we create a habit. This applies when we're altering a stressor, too – changing bad habits for good. So change your behaviour in order to feel more in control.

When you have a moment you can write down some of the stressors that you're experiencing. Some may be long-standing (like our harassed person with the unopened mail) as there are ways of behaving that have become entrenched and resulted in constantly fire-fighting. Some may be more recent stressors and some even more immediate.

It helps to write them down and to mark them according to the four classifications of: Accept, Adapt, Avoid, Alter.

Accept	Adapt	Avoid	Alter

Work out how you can change your *reactions* and the *situations* in order to relieve yourself of some of life's stress. You may have to 'mix and match' in order to solve the problem but there's no question that you'll be in a better place for having done so.

Be on alert at all times with your thinking and the way that you act (and react) and if you notice that you're blaming a situation or people for the way that you *feel*; pause and remind yourself of how emotions come into being. **Through your own thoughts**.

If you focus on *what* or *who* is the cause of your stressful situation and the problems you face, then:

● you take away the power you have to change things.

When you take the power back, then the focus changes to one of:

● changing a situation and solving a problem (as opposed to blame).

For example:

Angela:	'Natasha, would you just show the person who's over from Paris all the portfolios for the shoot relating to the new breakfast cereal commercial. She's in reception. Talk her through the campaign – you know the background. Must dash.'
Natasha (thinking):	'I've got to get this report out for the new perfume ad – I know I should have had it done by now, but I had to have two hours off on Tuesday for the dentist – why does she always land things on me? If I show this exec. all those portfolios I'll never get this perfume thing done – I know John needs this mid-morning tomorrow – if I stay late I'll miss Tanya's netball match – I promised her (*heart starts racing – feeling of anxiety*) – Angela's a nuisance – she did this once before on the day before Good Friday – didn't get a thanks, she just went off on holiday – why can't the executive from Paris come over at a less busy time?'

Take the control back to where it should be.

Negative cognitions are very powerful and determine your stress response. Put simply, you won't set off the stress response if your thoughts are of a positive 'I can handle this' nature. You will if your thinking says, 'I can't cope with this, what's happening . . .?' A whole load of emotions follow that set off a cycle that starts changes throughout your body, which become reinforced in a negative-feedback loop.

Toxic chemicals make 'toxic' thoughts

To recap: our thoughts are always generating emotions of a negative nature in response to our thoughts. Stressful thoughts also give rise to guilt, sadness, embarrassment, disappointment, remorse, envy, jealousy and more.

It's the 'chemical' stage that is interesting – and also the least understood by most people – inasmuch as it operates in a way that doesn't distinguish what particular negative emotion has been generated by your thinking.

So regardless of whether you're frightened or guilty or angry or embarrassed or sad or whatever, the same process occurs within the brain and body. It all happens in the endocrine (hormonal) system in conjunction with our nervous system.

The negative cognitions that find their way to the limbic system send messages along the neurons to the adrenal glands, stimulating many of the organs to increase their activity. These then release a number of different chemicals throughout the body and affect the pituitary gland, located under the hypothalamus (more on this in a moment).

Some important points about stress:

- As noted earlier, it triggers the fight/flight response.
- Our bodies are programmed to respond to our thoughts (as you saw in the last chapter) as though the event is happening in the *present*, regardless of whether the 'stressor' is caused by thinking about a *past* uncomfortable experience or anxiety about a *future* problem.
- Your body's 'pharmacy' will dispense the appropriate chemicals and hormones (as outlined in Chapter 1) 'now' – in the *present*.

Let's take a look at this mind–body connection. It will help you to recognise the physical symptoms that alert you to the fact that your fight-or-flight response is being activated.

It's always been said by scientists that our response to stress dates back to Neanderthal times and the dangers that were associated with everyday survival for our cave-dwelling ancestors. The bodies of our early ancestors reacted in the same way to emotion as ours do today, except that as we've noted the fight/flight reaction was of great benefit to them – literally life or death. It's a physiological response that activates a process enabling the mind and body to cope with the impending trauma. In addition it encodes a *memory* of an event so that we know we should avoid the situation another time ('I'm not going to that restaurant again. That ear-splitting music is just too loud. My heart's racing like an express train'). Or: 'I must avoid that stretch over there, that's where the pterodactyl seems to hang out' (I'm referring to prehistoric times now, not a Monday morning in Piccadilly).

For our ancestors, the main negative emotion was probably only fear; the stress chemicals provided energy to fight the bear or make a dash for it. This 'automatic arousal' response – as it's been termed – enabled the threatened to either fight or flee when confronted with danger from wild animals, other tribes or other obstacles to survival.

The difference between now and then is that for our ancestors, after fighting or fleeing, the body's parasympathetic nervous system switched off the supply of chemicals from the 'pharmacy' and then the physiological state gradually went back to normal.

Fine – in theory. In today's world we face a constant barrage of low-level stressors. Relentless. The fight/flight response is switched on more frequently than in days gone by.

Breaking the cycle

The reasons for much of our stress in modern society? Our emotions in the present day stretch to more than just fear. We have a multitude of emotions with which we burden ourselves. Take your pick: guilt, envy, regret, bitterness, frustration, to name a few. Fertile ground for negative thoughts.

For these constant thoughts we don't *need* the energy that those hormones have provided:

- and since we don't rid the body of these, they don't get a chance to exit our system;

- add to this the fact that we tend to cling onto the negative thoughts that are making us feel stressed;
- this tends to result in a cycle of negative thinking and self-defeating behaviour (as we saw in the last chapter);
- of course, the more time you spend thinking about your stressors, the more negative cognitions you have;
- and even more adrenaline, cortisol and other chemicals start pouring into the bloodstream;
- so you're constantly 'topped-up';
- the body's organs are working much faster than they should;
- you feel tired and exhausted in this stressed condition;
- your immune system also weakens.

The only remedy is to break this 'cycle'.

Today, our stressors are mainly psychological or social and do not require the same physiological assistance as in prehistoric times, but the body receives the same signals from the brain. Didn't you get a dry mouth during that presentation you gave last week? (See Chapter 5.)

Thankfully it's not so much the life-threatening situations we face now but more of just 'life'. And that's stressful enough. Most of our threats are psychological in nature.

Making it through the morning rush-hour without exploding, getting locked out of your house, your child coming home late, losing your wallet, being asked to write another report, confronting your boss at work, forgetting the key ingredient for a cake, waiting for medical test results, a long wait in a queue at the bank, fear of losing your job, increased petrol prices . . . where do we stop? These are typically the kind of 'threats' that face us in everyday life.

But they still activate our amygdala, those two small, almond-like regions of the fear circuit buried deep in the limbic area. They detect a threat or danger and make contact with the hypothalamus and instruct the fight/flight process to begin. Hormones, including the 'big two' – adrenaline and cortisol – start to flood our system. The amygdala also communicates with the 'movement' regions of the brain and after it has made its assessment, we'll either flee, prepare for 'fight' or 'freeze' (while we evaluate).

The key to trying to minimise our reactions to stress – and so calm the body down, before everything escalates – lies in our thinking and using techniques to relax the body.

Every time you encounter a 'perceived' threat your amygdala and your hypothalamus 'presses the buzzer' to set off the alarm and release a surge of the requisite hormones. It then passes a message to the brain centres dealing with fear and your mood state.

The main problem with the brain's message system to the body is that it's merely providing an alarm signal and not informing you about the particular danger that you're facing. So the body mobilises itself to fight a sabre-toothed tiger when the particular stressor you're facing happens to be the sight of the 9.22 to Manchester leaving the platform at King's Cross station ('Damn – I'll be late for that meeting now').

There's no doubt that all of us are subjected to categories of what we call 'major stressors' in life. Difficulties in these areas from time to time can drain our energy and contribute to a spiral of negative thoughts. Typically these are the 'big' ones:

- Relationship
- Work
- Health
- Family
- Finances
- Social life.

Just take a moment and glance at the list again. Is there one or more of these stressors that is occupying your thoughts almost constantly at the moment? (The nature of the 'big' ones is that the thoughts of these tend to be in the background most of the time.)

It is our perception of a particular situation that is responsible for stressful feelings that may engulf us. We may misinterpret other people's actions and form the wrong conclusions regarding their motives or we may be irrationally critical of our own performance.

Given what you now know about using the *MindControl* formula, how could you 'reframe' your thinking in one or more of those areas that we've identified? What irrational beliefs and negative cognitions are you able to 'dispute' and thereby control your thinking?

Take a few moments 'in your head' to just go through the formula. If it's a nagging stressor to do with a family matter, for example, what was the mental 'activator' (**M**) that triggered your irrational beliefs (**I**) leading to your negative cognitions (**N**)? Now 'dispute' (**D**) your line of thinking that serves only to increase your package of stress at this moment. Now that you've come up with a healthier way of looking at things – that serves you – you've taken control (**C**) of your state of mind.

The root of anxiety lies in fear. As we know, the physiological symptoms of breathing changes and rapid heartbeat are instant alarm signals that occur in the moment. On a more general level, we're engaged in the act of worrying. We need to know how to turn the body's alarm signal off and to recognise false alarms. Once again, we'll look at what's going on inside the brain which should help you in understanding the reason for the kick-start of the anxiety cycle (see Figure 4.1).

Remember the prefrontal cortex that we touched upon earlier? Just behind the eyes is the orbital frontal cortex (OFC). Hold on to that for a moment. Now, think of the amygdala – the fear centre of the brain. It sets off its alarm button as soon as it's primed for real threats as well as false ones. Either it works with the aid of the OFC or on its own.

Imagine that the amygdala is activated through three routes.

1 Via the cortex, which means that thought is involved.
   You're able to think about a situation before it translates into an anxious or fearful cognition. So you're able to rationally say

to yourself that things are okay and there's nothing to be fearful about. Equally, your irrational thoughts can tell you the opposite: that there is something to fear. (You can see how the dispute and control of *MindControl* are important here.)

2 Bypassing the cortex as the sympathetic nervous system (SNS) sets off the alarm system in the amygdala and makes you *feel* anxious before there's any *thought* (about what's making you feel that way). In a split second the norepinephrine activates the adrenal glands which flood epinephrine (adrenaline) into the bloodstream, increasing heartbeat, breathing and blood pressure – the fight or flight response.

3 You may remember the sequence whereby the amygdala sends a signal to the hypothalamus which tells the pituitary gland to tell the adrenal glands to start dispensing adrenaline and then cortisol. A chain of events known as the hypothalamus–pituitary–adrenal (HPA) axis comes into play.

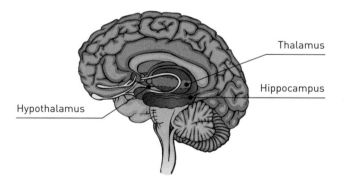

Figure 4.1 The hypothalamus, thalamus and hippocampus

Fitness for life

We spent a lot of time looking at the 'tortured' mind as it copes with modern day psychological stress. Well there's more and more evidence that aside from dealing with the stress chemicals in the body our happiness is enhanced by regular exercise. For the emotional and physical symptoms of the troubled mind, exercise is really effective treatment. It's an anti-anxiety treatment. Quite simply: changing the way you think combined with exercise is the most powerful way to lift your mood and bring a sense of joy.

With the fight/flight response that we looked at in some depth you'll remember that the problem is that the chemicals remain in our system – they have nowhere to go. Most threats that we face are 'psychological' dangers (notice that anger is danger without a '*d*') like anger and anxiety, as opposed to physical danger.

It used to be thought that exercise was good for our health because of its effect on the circulation and the heart. More and more research over the last decade or so has confirmed its cardiovascular benefits but has also shown the dramatic effects of increased oxygen in the brain, promoting the health of the capillaries (the small blood vessels).

When we engage in aerobic exercise – such as running, cycling, swimming, walking briskly – as well as exercising the heart and lowering blood pressure, the increased heart rate forces the blood into other areas of the body such as the arms and legs and so we're able to 'mop up' the excess of stress hormones and chemicals that have been languishing in the bloodstream. If left there, they cause us to think even *more* negative thoughts and rob us of happy moments. A hormone (peptide) that is produced as we increase our heart rate from exercise, reduces the stress response in our body since it halts the HPA axis (that we touched upon earlier) responsible for the fight/flight reaction. It also puts a brake on the stream of adrenaline.

What's significant about 'aerobic' (literally 'with air') exercise is its effect on the brain in that it produces:

- Neurotransmitters
- Beta-endorphins.

It produces those two neurotransmitters (depleted during the stress cycle) that elevate our mood and make us feel happy: noradrenaline and serotonin. The increased production of serotonin is generated when the body breaks down fatty acids in order to supply fuel to the muscles. Remember that a low level of serotonin in the body is linked to depression and anxiety.

Aerobic exercise also leads to an increase in our body's production of beta-endorphins. These natural morphines that the body produces also counter the effects of stress chemicals and improve our mood, making us feel energetic and optimistic. And as a natural 'opiate' produced by the body, it also helps to relieve pain. When you hear the term 'runner's high' it is because of the release of these endorphins into the bloodstream.

Much neuroscientific research continues into the additional benefit of exercise – apart from mood – relating to our brain's creativity and how it affects our learning capability. Because it boosts blood flow and the level of brain cell growth hormones, it encourages neuron growth. In the area relating to memory – the hippocampus – the research shows an increase in brain cell growth and a consequent improvement in learning ability. The studies into exercise also show a strengthening of the immune system. Even people diagnosed with depression have gained benefits and in some cases have avoided the need for antidepressants.

Coffee break . . .

 Stress invades our lives in a number of categories: relationship stress; work stress; money stress; parenting stress; general everyday stress.

 A stressful situation for one person may be thought of in a completely different way by another (pressure – or not even that). It's all to do with perception.

 The thalamus (in your limbic system) assesses the situation from the information coming into the brain and passes it onto the memory network in the amygdala (which stores memories of your previous emotional responses).

 There are four dimensions that are affected when pressure tips us into a stressful state: mental, emotional, physiological and behavioural.

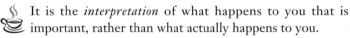 There is a physiological difference between perceived stress and perceived pressure. Higher levels of stress hormones are coursing through the bloodstream for the person under stress, compared with someone who feels pressured or just challenged (good enough reason to change your thinking).

 It is the *interpretation* of what happens to you that is important, rather than what actually happens to you.

 There are four techniques for dealing with stressful situations (the 4As): Adapt, Accept, Avoid, Alter.

The fight/flight activity (stress-response) is switched on in the body more frequently in the present day and two hormones, adrenaline and cortisol, tend to build up in the system.

Changing the way we think *combined* with exercise (ideally aerobic) is an ideal way to lift the mood – as all the research shows. The hormone peptide (produced from increased heart rate) puts a brake on the stream of adrenaline in the body and reduces the stress response by halting the HPA axis which is responsible for the fight or flight response.

Chapter

5

'My life has been full of terrible misfortunes, most of which never happened.'

Michel de Montaigne

Anxiety

We've seen how the mind-set of stress and the accompanying feelings can also lead to a physical effect on our bodies. The feelings are very powerful, as you've seen, and the negative thoughts that produce them are all too powerful. It is important to recognise that stress can also be caused by different emotions or moods. Just as thinking affects our moods, so moods can also affect our thinking.

As by now you know only too well that thoughts affect the way you feel, you'll understand that anxiety tends to arise out of thoughts that are related to being judged or coming to harm.

Feelings of anxiety usually involve a fixation on the **imagined future**, as opposed to what's happening in the 'now'. So we need to analyse and challenge our thinking in this, the present moment. Apart from feeling overwhelmed we may experience repeated episodes of uncontrollable worrying, a loss of objectivity and a pessimistic attitude of expecting the worst.

Our emotions drive our thinking just as powerfully as our thinking drives our emotions. This means none of us is a stranger to anxiety and fear. There are many definitions of these two overlapping terms and people tend to use them in a way that suggests they are interchangeable; for our purposes we'll treat them as the two ends of a spectrum. The common denominator is the word 'threat'. We feel threatened by something. When the threat goes, the anxiety goes.

Just one caveat. When people are fearful, sometimes there is an advantage in being anxious about the situation – we'll call this healthy anxiety (sounds like a contradiction); it keeps us alert about a possible upcoming situation. But most of the time the anxiety or fear is unhealthy.

An important point to reiterate here: **you can only hold one thought in your head at a time**.

Now that you know about the self-talk that is responsible for so much of our negative perceptions of situations, we can look at thoughts of fear and anxiety and reduce their debilitating effect on us. How essential is this? Well, when you consider surveys that show between 80 and 90% of what people worry about never actually materialises – very essential.

In fact it is the key to our well-being. How would you rather feel: anxious and depressed or happy and hopeful? Changing thoughts from the negative slant to a more positive one is again the key. Control, once again, is the prime need for the anxious person. People who are predisposed to an anxious nature will often cite their need to have control over things and events and consequently spend a lot of time trying to plan, arrange and pre-empt things. This makes life very stressful as you encounter that which cannot be controlled, which then feeds on the pre-existing anxiety or fears and compounds the negative mental state.

Real or imaginary?

As noted earlier, anxiety is usually triggered by a threat. Sometimes it's just a perceived one – about things in the future. Having to call David in next week to tell him there isn't the budget for a new computer system; daughter hasn't come back from the party yet, and she hasn't phoned; 1.30 train delayed due to points failure; conference speech coming up next week. These instances are often termed *state* anxiety as they cease to be a worry once the event has passed. We all tend to suffer from this type of anxiety.

Then there are people who seem to have almost a genetic pull towards a permanent state of anxiety. This is known as *trait anxiety*. A person like this is constantly focused on what could go wrong. They engage in many forms of 'distorted' thinking (as outlined in Chapter 2) and quite often are unable to enjoy life due to this pessimistic way of thinking. They may have an unhealthy need for control and try and reduce the uncertainties of life by trying to prevent the possibilities of things going wrong. Trying to achieve control over things that we can't hope to influence contributes to more anxiety. You can't hope to 'carpet' the world. You just have to learn to cope with whatever 'thinking skills' you can bring to each situation.

Experiences either in early life and/or later life can contribute to a disposition towards anticipating bad events. 'Disputing' thoughts (as in the *MindControl* model) is especially important for this type of person. There are people who suffer from a more serious type of anxiety disorder known as Generalised Anxiety Disorder (GAD) and they tend to need clinical attention.

Quite often our worry about specific events is unfounded; **they never happen**. Even if they do they may not be as bad as our 'cognitions' had led us to believe. So we spend a lot of time feeling anxious when there is no need – and even if things do happen, the worry will have contributed nothing. Except perhaps an agitated state, bodily imbalance and even ill-health.

It's often said that most people are more disturbed about the 'threat' of something happening in the future rather than misfortunes that actually occur. As Alfred Hitchcock said: 'There is no terror in the bang, only in the anticipation of it.'

We can handle 'real live' difficulties; it's the 'imaginary' ones that can't be conquered.

Worry afflicts us through the experience of:

- an external event – giving a presentation in a budget meeting at work next week; having to confront a relative or friend about an uncomfortable subject; or by
- a mental event – a particular thought that comes into our head.

This often sets a chain of thoughts in motion that are of the *'what if?'* family.

'What if they ask me about the training budget for Scotland? I won't have the figures for the North of England because we haven't done an analysis. They'll think I'm inefficient. What if the VP from Seattle is present? Suppose he expects all the figures in order to do a comparison?'

'I didn't realise I was that overdrawn on my bank account. Suppose the interest rates go up next year? I'll never be able to clear the balance. Suppose I break a leg or something? Being self-employed that would be disastrous. What if I can never work again? Who would look after Suzy? What about her piano lessons? She loves those. She'd never forgive me for the rest of her life – like that girl I saw talking about her mum on *Oprah* . . .'

And so the spiral continues!

Our anxiety is the *emotional* response to worry. We have the physical consequences and the psychological effects of irritability and lack of concentration. Anxiety appears as a consequence of worry – it builds on itself. So we don't look at tackling the consequence of worry, we look at what causes the spiral.

Some people seem to have the irrational belief that if you feel bad about something or just engage in long-term worry for long enough it changes something that happened in the past – or something that will happen in the future. Just by worrying and feeling bad! So the 'today' or the 'now' is eaten up with anxious thoughts. Worry doesn't clear out tomorrow of its possible problems, it abandons today, robbing it of its vitality.

There are two types of worry:

1 real problems which exist (real event);
2 problems that may exist.

This second type may never actually exist as *imagined*. These problems are often set in the distant future and are usually very unlikely to happen. They are often classed as hypothetical event worry. They have a habit of providing us with vivid images to accompany the 'soundtrack' in the mind that serves to create the illusion that the situation is real.

With real problems you can actually attempt to do something about them. You can 'think' rationally and try and solve the problem. This gives you a feeling of control. The trouble with the second type of worry is that as the subject of the worry is not necessarily going to happen and is in the future – what is there you can do? So all the mental energy is devoted to the actual worry itself – as opposed to thinking of a solution – creating a spiral.

For this type of worry, where the 'event' may never happen, it helps to rationalise thinking by considering:

1 On a scale of 1 to 10 how *likely* is it that the object of my worry will materialise?
2 If it happened could I *cope* with it?
3 If I *could*, what steps would I take?
4 Since I'm thinking about it so far in advance – I'm *prepared* for it.
5 What is most likely to *happen*?
6 What is the *best* thing that could happen?
7 If I can't handle it at the time: *what's the worst that could happen?*
8 Could I *get through* that?

By adopting this strategy, instead of constant worrying taking a big chunk of your 60,000–80,000 thoughts per day, you've dealt with the eventuality in your mind and prepared yourself for the consequences. And, more importantly, *it may never happen.*

Fear is usually more of a well-defined threat – something you're about to face. The monster in the wardrobe at two o'clock in the morning for the child; for the adult it may be stepping on to the podium to give a speech or the sound of a fire alarm. For our purposes we'll treat them as the same emotion. The common denominator is the word '**threat**'. We feel threatened by something.

When the 'threat' goes, the anxiety goes.

Feeling anxious or fearful gives rise to physical symptoms and unhelpful mental symptoms of worry, apprehension, helplessness and a cycle of negative thoughts.

We've been discussing thinking throughout the book and how disputing our thoughts and developing a healthier way of viewing situations changes our reaction to people and situations. If we can change our feelings by:

- disputing our thoughts of being anxious to a healthier state of *concern*;

- then this will change our *feelings* and then our *behaviour*.

Donna is asked if she'll be the 'auctioneer' at the school's charity auction along with another parent, Madeleine.

Donna has done some 'public speaking' in the past but becomes anxious nearing the time of the event. Madeleine has never had to face people in a situation like this ('The last time was when I was in a debating society at university when I was 18' was her original protest – before accepting). However, Madeleine's looking forward to it, and feels it will be fun – she's just healthily *concerned* that she handles things okay. But she knows that Donna will be there, too, sitting in the front row, if she gets stuck.

Donna, however, has the irrational belief that whilst she has survived speaking in a public situation before, this time it will all end badly ('Suppose I forget what the last person has bid – it all moves so fast. It'll be humiliating if I do, with all those parents there. What will they think? It would be awful if I came out with the wrong figure . . .'). So right up to the day of the auction she has been in a state of anxiety whilst Madeleine has been looking forward to 'a bit of fun' and 'the wine and cheese' afterwards.

So the two women were faced with a 'threat' but the anxiety-related belief meant that Donna was anxious about the charity auction whilst Madeleine, who had a healthier concern-related belief, did not regard the situation as a threat and therefore did not suffer from anxiety and was focused on her performance (and a glass or two of wine!).

If we look at the two points of view and you can think back to those 'distorted' thinking habits that we all engage in from time to time, you'll notice that one of Donna's beliefs is 'It would be awful if I . . .'. If she brings just that one belief to the situation (let alone all the other 'clues' about her other distorted interpretations!) then when she sets out to perform the task her focus would be on that – the threat. Consequently, she's not thinking about the purpose of being there – and her performance may suffer.

Madeleine, on the other hand, thinks in a different way. She's had less experience in a public arena but brings no specific beliefs to the situation – in other words, no general anxiety-related beliefs. She doesn't focus on whether she'll do the job well; or not so well; her focus is on the actual job she has 'volunteered' for and what she needs to know in order to handle it. Consequently she sees no threat in the situation and is not anxious before the event. She brings a healthy level of concern – enough to motivate her – on the day and looks forward to the auction and having a pleasant time (since she's giving up her Saturday).

Donna's daughter – on hearing that her mother, a few days before the auction, was going to back out and give her excuses as to why she couldn't do it – took her in hand.

'Look, Mum, if you're worried about forgetting how much the last bid was, can't you just quickly jot down each figure as it's shouted at you – you don't even have to look down at the paper – then if the last figure slips your mind, it's there. Nobody cares, what's awful about it? It's only other mums and dads and relatives and friends who are there.'

On the day, as it happens, everything goes well. The two women collect a record amount of auction takings (and afterwards they both consume a record amount of white wine).

Let's take a look at what this situation highlights. An upcoming event generated anxiety and concern, for Donna and Madeleine respectively. Anxiety and concern are usually about *future* events. When we have these feelings it's because we consider that we are facing some kind of threat. If you hold certain anxiety-inducing beliefs then if you are facing a particular threat you will feel anxious. Another person who has concern-inducing beliefs about a situation will, when confronted with the same threat, just be concerned as opposed to anxious. Who has the better time?

We can say that when we change our thinking to one of concern, we're in a less intense situation than when we feel anxious and can look at – and deal with – things in a more constructive way and, more importantly, remain in control.

Let's take our *MindControl* model to look at Donna's thinking:

M (mental activator):	Chosen to be one of the auctioneers.
I (irrational belief):	'I may not remember the bids. What will they *think* of me? I wouldn't be able to stand the humiliation of coming out with the wrong figure . . .'
N (negative emotional consequences):	Anxiety right up to the day of the auction. Was about to back out a few days before (now that would have been more *humiliating* . . .) before the pep talk from her daughter.

D (dispute):	**'What's humiliating about it? Who said you were a professional auctioneer? What's wrong with writing down each figure you hear (thanks to your daughter)? It's not Sotheby's in New York – it's a school auction for charity!'**
Control (thinking):	**'I'm going to enjoy this in a few days' time. I'm sure I'll handle this well. I'll jot down each bid and concentrate on maximising the proceeds for each item by being confident. Let's see if we can break records.'**

(Since Donna didn't activate the fight/flight response – with none of those damaging stress chemicals coursing through her bloodstream – her body language and her confident communication led to a record-breaking day.)

By changing her thinking Donna experienced no anxiety for the six days leading up to the event. Remember: her feelings of being anxious were because of her unhealthy beliefs about the threat. Donna was worried about a threat to her *self-esteem* (more about that later). Madeleine, on the other hand, was just concerned that she knew enough about the procedure of how the event would be run, in order to be confident of carrying out her duties.

I just want to refer back to our example. At one stage Donna was thinking of backing out of the task that she'd been assigned (look back to N in *MindControl*). Here she was exhibiting one of the behavioural consequences of what people do when facing anxiety. Either you act in a way to cope with your anxiety or you can behave in a way so that you don't experience it – in other words, you'll take yourself away from the threat. In Donna's case she was engaging in *avoidance*.

This is a behavioural consequence that is common when people want to avoid a situation that they regard as a threat. Fine for the short-term, but it does nothing for your confidence or self-esteem because, as you haven't challenged your thinking, it only serves to *reinforce* your beliefs – ready to crop up *again* in a similar situation.

It's only a thought;
it can't hurt you

Any kind of avoidance provides a relief at the time. To the mind it provides a *reward* and so quite naturally you get used to avoiding 'uncomfortable' situations. You feel good each time. But it stops you from stretching yourself after a while. It stops you from taking risks, chances, and putting yourself in situations that can lead to your goals and dreams.

It's far better to *challenge* your existing beliefs and look at things from a different angle.

Remember these points:

- when the *perception* of a threat disappears – the *anxiety* disappears. And of course, in most cases, it is nothing more than a perception;
- we can change our thinking to be *concerned* about a 'threat' rather than be *anxious* about it.

The mind–body connection

Let's take a look at this mind–body connection in some detail. It will help you to recognise the physical symptoms that alert you to the fact that your fight-or-flight response is being activated.

The root of anxiety lies in fear. As we know, the physiological symptoms of breathing changes and rapid heartbeat are instant alarm signals that occur in the moment. On a more general level we're engaged in the act of worrying. We need to know how to turn the body's alarm signal off and to recognise false alarms. Once again, we'll look at what's going on inside the brain, which should help you in understanding the reason for the kick-start of the anxiety cycle.

Let's recap the reasons for much of our anxiety in modern society.

Our emotions in the present day stretch to more than just fear. We have a multitude of emotions with which we burden ourselves. Take your pick:

- Guilt
- Envy
- Regret
- Bitterness
- Frustration
- Shame
- Anger.

These are just a few. All provide fertile ground for negative thoughts. We don't need the energy that the resulting hormones have provided – and since we don't rid the body of these, they don't get a chance to exit our system.

When we've experienced a true fight/flight situation (as opposed to psychological 'threat'), the body's parasympathetic nervous system (PNS) switched off the supply of chemicals from our 'pharmacy' and then the physiological state gradually levelled out. The body's stress-response system has an inbuilt facility for returning things to normal after the particular threat has gone away. The two hormones – adrenaline and cortisol – that initiated a faster heart rate and increased blood pressure, having done the job, now fall and the body returns to normal as all the other elements of the system go back to their usual physiological state.

If not yourself, how many people do you know or observe – both in personal and work life – who are perpetually tense, anxious or nervous and therefore feel stressed the whole time?

Our nervous system governs our bodily responses and this is subdivided into what's termed the voluntary nervous system (also known as the somatic system), that relates to the nerves linked to the muscles that control our movement and our senses. Then we have our autonomic nervous system (ANS), the nerves that connect to our various organs and glands, in charge of the 'automatic' activities that we take for granted – like digestion and breathing.

The ANS is split into two, namely the **sympathetic** and **parasympathetic** functions:

1 The sympathetic is in charge of the fight or flight response. It mobilises the body very quickly to deal with the threat in one of the two ways.

2 The parasympathetic function is responsible for returning the system to its previous state. So all the 'resting' functions such as breathing and digestion return to normality.

When the sympathetic function goes in the 'on' position, the following happens.

Your hypothalamus (see Chapter 4) transmits messages to the adrenal glands – located above the kidneys – to secrete various hormones, the two important ones being:

● **Adrenaline** – responsible for accelerated heartbeat and raised blood pressure.

● **Cortisol** – this is the main stress hormone that elevates the glucose (sugars) in the blood and halts functions that are not needed in fight or flight, such as the digestive system.

You'll probably be familiar with some of these 'sympathetic' physical responses prompted by the release of these chemicals by the brain:

● Increase in muscle tension mobilising you for action.

● Digestive tract goes into shutdown mode and so provides extra blood for the other muscles.

● Mouth often becomes dry due to less saliva. The digestive system suppression leads to less gastric juices in the body.

- Liver releases extra glucose for quick energy.
- Pupils dilate (better view of 'danger').
- Heart beats faster (this pumps more blood to the muscles for running or fighting).
- Breathing more rapid and deeper, providing more oxygen to the lungs.

A word about the last item in the list above: breathing. Because we tend to take it for granted, we're quite often unaware of the powerful effects of breathing and what it does to the brain – and consequently the effect it has on our thinking.

Pause for breath . . .

When we breathe faster or deeper – or both – and it is more than is required by the body to cover its demands for oxygen and the removal of carbon dioxide, it results in *hyperventilation*. Put simply, this is overbreathing. It leads to a loss of carbon dioxide in the blood – not a good thing since carbon dioxide is a key player in maintaining a certain pH level and is used by the body to regulate our breathing.

In a state of hyperventilation the pH levels are therefore raised in our nerve cells and activate the fight or flight condition, leading to the physical symptoms described above. The situation is compounded because most people are unaware that they are hyperventilating – because many of us take breathing for granted. A cycle begins as the more anxious they get, the more anxious they get.

Overbreathing is usually to do with one or two breathing patterns: upper chest breathing, instead of from the diaphragm, is often a cause. This type occurs when:

- the chest lifts upward and outward;
- breathing becomes rapid and also shallow.

A lot of people who have long-term anxiety problems develop a habit of upper chest (thoracic) breathing and it becomes their 'default' pattern of breathing. Others, when they become anxious in a particular situation, will instinctively resort to this type of breathing. Why we do this is difficult to answer. What is clear is that the resulting chemical change causes a chain reaction that prepares us for crisis.

Diaphragmatic breathing is characterised by:

- slower and deeper breathing;
- as they become full of air the lower part of the lungs push down on the diaphragm;
- this causes the abdominal region to protrude and the stomach expands and then contracts (with the rhythm of the breath).

This type of breathing is a relaxed form that we use if we're not engaging in any form of physical activity. However, some people spend a large part of their waking hours breathing from the upper body as they try to cope with everyday 'threatening' situations. Unless they change their cognitions – nothing changes.

An added problem in modern society and with 'celebrity culture' is the need to look good, be slim, and have flat stomachs and 'six-packs' (for men). The tendency to hold the stomach in and tense the abdominal muscles whilst sitting, standing or walking (that doesn't leave much else!) means that diaphragmatic breathing is not possible and so thoracic area breathing becomes the standard way of operating. Add in tight-fitting clothes as another hazard for some people and there's even more of society unconsciously using this type of breathing.

So how much of the mild anxiety symptoms that people experience are being exacerbated by their breathing patterns? **Changing your breathing habit will change your thoughts**.

Let's observe your 'default' way of breathing (please do this when you have a convenient moment – it will pay dividends):

1 Take a deep breath while you have one hand on your chest and the other on your stomach.

2 Which hand moved the most?

3 If it was your hand on the chest – you're breathing from the thoracic area and so you're exhibiting **upper-chest** breathing.

4 This means that you're overbreathing and it's producing some of the fight/flight symptoms – in varying degrees – in everyday life (try being aware of relaxed breathing).

5 If the hand on your stomach moved the most – **diaphragmatic** breathing. This is a healthier way of breathing (try and keep this up in tense situations).

Remember that our emotions in the present day stretch to more than just anxiety and fear. We have a multitude with which we burden ourselves: guilt, envy, regret, bitterness, frustration, to name a few. Fertile ground for negative thoughts. These are typically the kind of 'threats' that face us in everyday life.

The key to trying to minimise our reactions to these stressful events – and so calm down, before everything escalates – lies in our thinking and using techniques to relax the body.

Remember that it is our perception of a particular situation that is responsible for anxious and fearful feelings that may engulf us. We may:

● misinterpret other people's actions;

● worry about the threat of future events (and form the wrong conclusions);

● be irrationally critical of our own performance.

Given what you now know about using the *MindControl* formula, think of some anxious feelings that are on your mind at the moment. Which category do they come under? How could you 'reframe' your thinking in one or more of those areas that we've identified? Are you able to 'dispute' some irrational beliefs and negative cognitions and therefore control your thinking? Take a few moments to just go through the formula.

As mentioned earlier, if you have the opportunity to casually jot down your thoughts it helps you to focus. You can then spend time looking at the words you've used to describe the situation, which is often very telling. Just seeing the words helps the 'disputing' stage.

Remember these points:

- When the *perception* of a threat disappears – the *anxiety* disappears. And of course, in most cases it is nothing more than a perception.

- We can change our thinking to be *concerned* about a 'threat' rather than *anxious* about it.

Sometimes looking at the funny side of life gives us a better perspective on things. A good sense of humour is a perfect antidote to stress and anxiety.

See if there's a humorous side to what's happening – maybe it would be funny if you were watching it happen to somebody else!

So look for the humour. Like the art thief who dumped his van by the side of the road (after running out of petrol) containing his haul from the art gallery – leaving this note on the windscreen for the police:

> **I didn't have any MONET**
> **in order to buy DEGAS**
> **to make the VAN GOGH.**
> **Merci beaucoup CONSTABLE.**

Coffee break . . .

 Feelings of anxiety usually involve a fixation on the imagined future – as opposed to what's happening in the 'now'.

 Control is often a prime need of the anxious person – control over things and events. This leads to an excessive amount of time spent in trying to arrange, plan and pre-empt things, making life very stressful.

 Generally there are two types of anxiety that are prevalent: **trait** anxiety and **state** anxiety. Trait anxiety is a state where a person is on constant alert of what could go wrong; they engage in almost constant 'distorted' thinking (as discussed in Chapter 2). State anxiety is usually about things that cease to be a worry when the event has passed (common to all of us).

 We often worry about things that are unfounded – they never happen. Or they're not as bad as our cognitions had led us to believe. So a lot of time is spent being anxious when there is no need.

 There are two types of worry: real problems that exist (real event) and problems that may exist (hypothetical event).

 We can generally handle 'real life' difficulties; it's the 'imaginary' ones that can't be conquered.

Fear leads to avoidance, which is fine at the time as it provides the mind with a reward, but it stops you from taking chances and risks. It does nothing for your confidence or self-esteem and serves to reinforce beliefs.

Anxiety of a long-term nature often leads to upper chest (thoracic) breathing. The more relaxed diapraghmatic breathing, which is slower and deeper, is more desirable.

Changing your breathing changes your thoughts.

Look for the humour in any situation – it gives a better perspective on things.

Chapter 6

'Before you judge a man, walk a mile in his shoes.
After that who cares? He's a mile away and you've
got his shoes.'

Billy Connolly

Anger

We'll now look at the second element of psychological stress that arises when we perceive a situation of threat or danger: anger. It's an emotional response that activates the fight/flight response with which you're now very familiar. Sometimes what we perceive as anger is in fact not 'true' anger but stress. For example: 'No, I don't want a cup of coffee. How many times? Now will you just leave me for a moment, I've got to get this e-mail sent by 7 o'clock.' This kind of talk is from a person who is stressed – anger is their way of *conveying* it.

Everything we've covered so far has been related to our beliefs and attitudes which determine the way we think. As you know, it is not events that disturb you but the view that you take of them. Similarly with anger – no one can *make* you angry. You can't pin the responsibility for your emotions on another person or a situation.

They don't have the power. You have the power. The *mind power*. Our anger is very much a personal thing. It helps if we can put ourselves in the other person's shoes sometimes; to 'walk a mile in their shoes' as the saying goes. To try and observe a situation from the other person's perspective. Keep this caveat in mind and as you are confronted with situations, programme your mind to give you a jolt.

Of course the amount of stress that you have in your life will determine your predisposition to frequent angry outbursts or longer-term anger. The usual stress-related illnesses are a danger as stress *causes* anger and anger *causes* stress. The feedback loop means when we're experiencing stress, either acute or chronic, we're more likely to find ourselves having outbursts of anger as our tolerance levels become more fragile – therefore causing more stress. More stress then causes more anger.

Small things that normally would pass without incident can incite a hostile reaction. Bringing home stress from work can turn the most trivial domestic problem into a catastrophe. This 'displaced' anger is a common feature of everyday life. You see it on the roads – typically as drivers show their rage as they displace stresses from other areas of their lives.

As in all the other situations we've looked at, the *external* activator that leads to your anger may well have provided you with an opportunity to be angry. It's up to you whether you want to take it. You can choose to be angry, fly into a rage or whatever – but it's your choice. When you find yourself thinking or saying things like:

- 'The electrician put me in such a foul mood yesterday . . .'
- 'He's ruined the lunch now . . .'
- 'They force me to shout at them . . .'

it takes the control away from you (making you 'hold on' to thoughts) and suggests that your emotions are owned by other people. You are reacting in a certain way which is a feeling of anger. Rephrase your thoughts or dialogue to bring control back to you or you will feel at the mercy of events. To repeat – it's not events that disturb you, it's your reactions.

How different do you feel if you rephrase the preceding statements with:

- 'I was so angry with the electrician for being late and forgetting the fittings . . .'
- 'I didn't enjoy the lunch because he introduced the topic of last Christmas . . .'
- 'I end up having to raise my voice to get them to do things . . .'

You've taken control of the situation now; these are your new responses (as opposed to reactions) to the situation. After all:

- The electrician didn't put you in a foul mood – you felt angry because you weren't able to get to the shops, because he was late arriving. Also you wanted the fittings installed that week.

- Your guest didn't actually ruin the meal. You felt uncomfortable discussing the topic and so you didn't enjoy the lunch.

- You feel they'll only cooperate if you shout at them.

We'll be looking at ways you can suspend your immediate reactions later.

It's noticeable that most people fail to take into account the fact that everybody has a different reality. Remember what we paused to assimilate earlier on: there is no such thing as 'reality', only perception. Your subjective view of the world will be different to another person's. Attempt to take that on board in the split seconds before you give in to an angry impulse and also try to see something from the other person's point of view when you're on the *receiving* end.

So it's when we perceive something to be not right that we may experience this emotion of anger. As with anxiety, discussed in the previous chapter, it is usually associated with a perception of *threat* or *danger*. The stress-fight- (from our flight/fight) emotional response is anger, and of course when we're in physical danger this is a useful reaction. But we have to remember that a lot of anger is not generated in situations like these.

Although the connotations are negative, if handled appropriately and at the right intensity, anger can make things happen. Yet anger is such a personal thing it's quite often difficult for us to put ourselves in the other person's shoes when things get out of hand.

Think about it. Your son has the music up too loud and insists on putting his feet up on the sofa – and his shoes have been in the paddocks that morning. Despite asking him twice, calmly, to turn down the music and remove his feet from the sofa – nothing. Then you storm in, iron in hand, and pull the plug out of the mains, hand on hips:

'How many times? I've got a headache from not enough sleep – having to get your stuff washed and ironed by tomorrow for your school trip. I can't hear myself think. Now you want me to wash the sofa covers as well, from your shoes full of manure – I've got nothing better to do of course!'

'Sorry, Mum – err, I'll get out your way now.'

This kind of scene is played out – even as you're reading it – all over the planet every day. It's a display of low-level anger. You do the same kind of thing if you're returning a faulty item to a store and they fail to acknowledge your inconvenience and point of view. You show your irritation, your displeasure, your annoyance – these are all forms of anger. You leave the store after having assertively made your point and achieved the outcome you desired.

We engage in this kind of behaviour all the time in our personal and working lives. The problem with anger is that it's associated with its extreme form – rage. This is anger at the high end of the spectrum. Moreover, it's associated with destructive actions and so understandably it's regarded as an unhealthy emotion with negative consequences. And of course at its high end, anger triggers all those undesirable chemicals and bodily sensations that we've been considering.

Since we're looking at the process of how your thinking may result in anger that is not a rational response to a situation, let's summarise the two instances in which it is the wrong response:

1 When there is **no** threat that needs to be dealt with.

2 When the level of anger is **inappropriate** for the situation that 'activated' it.

When this happens it is either due to a person's beliefs based on their distorted way of thinking (we looked at a lot of those in Chapter 2) or to their mental state at the time – stressed in other words, for whatever reason.

Much anger is a negative influence in people's lives if:

- it's too intense;
- it occurs on a regular basis;
- it lasts too long.

Much of what we have to deal with in everyday life comes under the category of being 'annoyed' or 'irritated', which is way down the anger scale. By definition these feelings, which are frequent in occurrence, tend to just come and go. As such they are much healthier and a change of thinking – with practice, of course – can help us downgrade an incident from creating an angry feeling to one of annoyance or irritation. *MindControl*. Dispute your interpretation.

Dealing with short-term and long-term anger

Psychologists, researchers and neuroscientists have spent a lot of time analysing the causes, effects and different types of anger. They've identified two distinct types:

1 Transient (or short-term) anger

2 Long-lasting anger.

With transient anger we're talking about a *situational* type. The person has a short burst of anger (or rage) and all the visible physiological signs show themselves in a matter of seconds and then everything calms down quickly. Of course it's the repercussions that are the problem in this situation. The explosion may be short term but the effects on others may be long term. Relationships between partners, work colleagues, friends, children, clients, can all be damaged – in a matter of seconds.

Even prime ministers have felt the long-term damage of an angry outburst – vented in the comfort and privacy of their own ministerial car (or so they think). But they need to remember to turn off their microphone after having given radio interviews!

We feel anger against people a lot of the time but also against organisations, situations, governments and the world. Not all anger is bad of course. If we didn't feel angry about things at times then we wouldn't have the motivation to try and change things. If it's appropriate to the situation and done in the right way, for the right reasons, then expressing this emotion is valid and helpful.

With long-lasting anger the root cause is an unhealthy/ 'distorted' way of thinking whereby there is an expectation about people and the world and that things should be different. An expectation that people should or should not have behaved in a different way and, as Albert Ellis put it, constant *ruminating* (He said . . . then I said . . . then guess what he said . . . so I said . . . and then she butts in and says . . . and I said, 'Excuse me . . .').

We all know about resentments that can last for years or over a whole lifetime. A change of thinking is the only way out of this scenario as it clouds a person's emotions over a long period and takes up precious mental time, with a spiral that leads to the same thought destination.

Let's get one thing straight first of all, to put it into perspective. Anger is a feeling just like feelings we have of joy, sadness, anxiety, resentment, for example. As with those feelings, it's our thinking that drives the emotions. Anger comes from our own thoughts about a situation.

Of course, it's other people's actions that are the mental activators (M) for our anger, but our reaction will be determined by how we choose to *perceive* things. So as we've learnt, we can control our feelings by controlling our thinking. Scientists have observed that anger differs from other unhealthy emotions in that there is a tendency to not want to let go of it. It seems that our sense of justice at certain times may be so strong that we want to continue with the feelings and not let the other person (or thing) 'get away with it'. It's easy to rationalise it when we say to someone: 'But you're suffering by holding on to the anger.'

How many people do you know who are in this position? I mean suffering. They're holding on – terrier-like – to their lifelong feuds, feeling good and feeling bad at the same time. Feeling good that they're not letting the person off for their past misdemeanours and feeling bad at the same time. And you know – in the battle of the mind – who always wins in the battle of the positive and negative spiral? Well, if you remember, the mind doesn't 'do' positive spiral. Doesn't exist. The spiral is always downwards and negative thoughts win the battle.

So: if you consider it makes you feel 'good' when holding on to a feud. What's the downside? Surely the 'bad' overshadows the good? These are different people's comments:

- When I think about it, I get upset (gives me stress headaches).

- Have to 'avoid' them when I see them in the street (causes me discomfort and stress).

- I wake up at night – sometimes I have dreams and think about it; goes round and round in my head (feel emotional and exhausted from loss of sleep).

- I find it exhausting when I have discussions with others about the situation (fatigue).

- Depriving ourselves of a friendship – makes me sad as well as angry (waste of life).

So what can we do to minimise unhealthy anger when it is caused by our thinking?

Minimising anger

I recommend the following approach which gives you time to think – as opposed to reacting inappropriately. Bearing in mind that if you are prone to angry outbursts – whether irrational or not – it will by now be habitual behaviour and you will have to gradually replace it with this alternative 'habit':

1. Cease – cool – count

At the first sign of angry thoughts in your mind.

Cease thinking – your automatic thoughts are not likely to be rational and helpful so put a stop to them quickly.

Cool – bring your mental temperature down and think 'cool'.

Isn't it the easiest thing in the world to 'lose your cool'? Your intuitive reaction to an event may generate feelings of anger as the autonomic nervous system makes an interpretation of an impending threat or danger. How many times have you said to yourself that a situation would have been better served by your cool and rational behaviour which would have brought the temperature down. But no. It's easier to do the opposite. In other words, to *react*.

You might ask – what's wrong with reacting? Well – when we're angry we tend to react. We're slaves to our emotions.

It's far better to *respond*.

> **When we respond: *we're* controlling the mind – instead of the mind controlling *us*.**

Instead of being fixated on the anger-inducing situation that we're experiencing (the cause), if we focus on our internal response we're effectively deciding the severity of the anger and how long it will last and, more importantly, how we *behave*.

Life's too serious to be taken too seriously

It's our behaviour when we're out of control that gets us into trouble and leads to us constantly having to issue apologies and endure fractured relationships. It's a habit that has to be broken and if it's ingrained – as many long-held habits inevitably are – it will take practice. It pays enormous dividends and if you're to have a better and more stress-free life it's worth the change. So, if you recognise yourself as belonging to this category make an effort to replace your habit with the healthier one: to *respond* rather than *react*.

> **When you *react* to feelings of anger you're *out of control*.**
> **When you *respond* to feelings of anger you're *in control*.**

Why is this? Because:

> **When you react to feelings of anger you're**
> **engaging in a *reflex* action.**
> **When you respond to feelings of anger you're**
> **engaging in *thinking*.**

1. Count

Counting from one to ten in your mind is still one of the best disciplines. It's amazing how the mere act of distracting yourself 'cognitively' can defuse a situation, as it reminds you that you want to achieve a certain outcome – as well as venting your emotions. It allows you to make a quick evaluation of whether what you were either going to *say* ('Don't you even dare think that . . .') or *do* (throw that glass of red wine over their new suit) will serve your purpose.

Note: sometimes you are better served by physically leaving the situation – especially if you need more time to collect your thoughts. Since the negative emotions (anger) are connected with the situation, breaking away *geographically* tends to dilute the emotions. You think better. And as you know – how you think is how you feel.

So 'regroup' and 'reframe' – leave the situation until you're in a better state so that you can reframe your thinking, freeing it from distortions and changing it for a more rational approach that will lead to a better outcome and preserve relationships.

Have you seen those TV documentaries filmed in airports – those angry outbursts at check-in desks? The people that are content to rant and rage and demand and finally be abusive. Then there are the passengers that walk away after an initial angry outburst. They leave the scene and then return – with a more rational head. You are able to control your temper. The choice lies with you.

2. Analyse the anger

Engage in self-talk and say to yourself: 'What's the reason for my anger?'

Naturally the finger points to the 'trigger' or 'activator' that has aroused your angry feelings. But is that always the case? Sometimes it's far removed from the actual situation in which we find ourselves.

Don't we all have things that are sometimes 'stewing' in the mind? Or maybe we're on the cusp of the 'pressure cooker' state, when it just takes one little stressor that pushes us over the edge. The result is that the intensity of the anger may be inappropriate and the people at whom the onslaught is directed may be innocent.

At other times you may want to ask yourself: 'What do I want out of this situation?'

Instead of revenge or making the other person or organisation feel bad, you may ultimately want something specific. It may be monetary, it may be an apology or it may just be an acknowledgement of poor behaviour or service. Are you jeopardising achieving your ultimate aim by an angry outburst – when *you* may end up being the one apologising (instead of the other party)?

Sometimes you have to consider: 'Is it worth it?'

Is it worth expending emotional energy – especially if it's an awkward situation – only for you to be left with the legacy of all those bodily changes to your nervous system, that all go 'up' when you're involved in an angry confrontation? If it's just a case of letting another person or organisation know about your unhappiness, perhaps it can be done in a calmer way. If you feel strongly about something (poor service in a restaurant, for example) it's better not to suppress your anger. You can be angry without triggering your fight/flight response. When you speak, instead of sounding out of control, modulate your voice and deliver your message in an assertive (instead of aggressive) fashion.

3. Does the anger fit the situation?

Quite often when we do a 'post-mortem' on an angry exchange that we've had with someone or we're experiencing general angry feelings that are putting us into an unpleasant mood, we'll conclude that it was not the right reaction. So always check with yourself: 'Is it appropriate?' Because most things are subjective we can be realistic and suggest that most situations are a mixture of both appropriate and inappropriate anger.

This helps in gaining a rational viewpoint, because much anger is due to 'something else'. We might be tired, hungry, suffering from an illness or stressed. As to this last one, we know that stress causes anger.

I was given an instance by somebody who related to me how she flew into a rage because the two assistants in the department store were animatedly talking about *Strictly Come Dancing* and ignoring her (the customer). (She was already running late for an appointment.)

It generated a lot of drama as customers and staff from other counters looked on as she shouted at them ('. . . don't forget it's customers that pay your salaries . . .'). A manager eventually arrived and calmed her down and served her with the moisturising cream. The trouble was, she told me, she was so agitated and also so embarrassed as she hurriedly left the store that she dropped some of the banknotes (her change from the £50 note) that she had quickly pushed – with her gloved hand – into her coat pocket with the receipt. She just wanted to get out of the store.

The result was that her fight/flight activities kept her in a bad state for the whole day as she constantly replayed the events in her head, generating more anger as those stress chemicals took hold.

Was there any particular reason that she blew up, I asked her? Was she able to analyse her thinking, in the cold light of day? 'Yes, if I think about,' she said. 'I felt stressed because I was already running late for an appointment.'

Sometimes we have to look at the effect that our actions can produce. A change of thinking of the 'is it worth it?' or 'what do I want out of this?' variety may be the better option. We may have the satisfaction of berating the accused – because they've caused us to be late for an appointment – but we're left with the consequences of our rage. Counting to ten may have helped that person suppress her rage. A healthier conversation showing her *annoyance* with the two store assistants would have left her in a better state physiologically – and a little richer!

4. Decide on what action to take

As the root of anger is some kind of threat. What this last stage is concerned about is some kind of healthy and positive behaviour that we can engage in to lessen or dissipate the threat. Sometimes it's a change of thinking – other times a change of behaviour. In our earlier example in the department store, the customer could perhaps have asked for the manager and conveyed her annoyance about the situation. She would still have made her point in an assertive way as opposed to an aggressive way.

It's still remarkable how many people have not stopped to consider the difference between assertiveness and aggression. They're most certainly not the same thing even though in each case the object is to be successful in securing needs and wants and being sure about and standing up for one's rights.

Dealing with situations in an assertive way means that situations, relationships and conflicts are dealt with in a way that is satisfactory for both parties. Agreement and solutions are the aims with assertive behaviour; with the rights and respect of both sides taken into account. Conversely, interactions conducted in an aggressive way are one-way; with the requirements of the other side pushed aside.

So handling your anger is, as you can see, handling your perceptions. Your thoughts, as always, are driving your emotions. Can you recall a recent bout of anger (last seven days) that affected you? How did you cool down? Did you make allowances for the person/situation? Did that rational thought help you choose your words better?

Think back – how much of the anger was based on the ubiquitous 'should' rule that we impose in life? 'Shoulds' about people, situations and the world? We know that our lack of flexibility by imposing too many of these on situations leads to our emotions taking over (**thinking–feeling–behaviour**) and leading to a loss of control on our part. I often think that it's time for a new advertising slogan to replace the 'Image is everything' one. Well, here it goes (note to advertising agencies: you know how to get hold of me). Let's bring it out into the open: '*Control is everything.*'

It's worth repeating the point that as you own the anger, you make the decision as to whether to engage in this emotion. Yes, of course other people or situations or life generally will delight in taunting us so that we reach the 'tipping point' for an angry outburst. But, whichever way we look at a situation, it falls to us to decide how we manage our own anger – since we control our own responses.

On a final note, sometimes it's worth just stepping back and deciding whether something is worth the mental and emotional turmoil that excessive anger entails. Wasting time over prolonging anger instead of looking at alternative ways of thinking. Being too serious for the sake of it. After all, **life's too serious to be taken too seriously**.

Aristotle (384–322 BC) put it well all that time ago:

'Anybody can become angry – that is easy, but to be angry with the right person and to the right degree at the right time and for the right purpose, and in the right way – that is not within everybody's power and is not easy.'

Perhaps the man below needs a dose of Aristotle's philosophy – I'm sure his wife would agree!

A man and his wife leave a motorway service station and after about 15 minutes of driving:

Patricia: 'Don – stop. Now! Over there – stop there.'

Don: 'What is it? What's wrong?'

Patricia: 'My specs – I've left them at the service station. On the table – where we had breakfast . . . I think.'

Don: (in a thunderous voice): 'What? We've got to drive all the way back. And it's just started to rain. Why can't you look when you leave a table? Honestly . . .'

Patricia: 'I do normally. I was distracted when the waitress asked if I had a ten pound note instead of twenty – they were short of change.'

Don: 'I don't care. You're always leaving things behind somewhere.'

Patricia: 'Always? Twice including this. I suppose you never leave things in shops or restaurants or wherever.'

Don: 'As it happens I don't. Now we've got to find a b****** slip road to turn back. You are such a pain . . .'

Throughout the journey back, Don is in a foul mood – blood pressure rising – and has intermittent angry outbursts. He continually chides Patricia for her 'always' leaving things. Less than 20 minutes later they arrive back at the service station. Patricia gets out of the car and is about to open her umbrella and dash over to the entrance of the cafeteria when Don shouts over to her through the half-opened window:

'While you're in there you might as well get my mobile phone.'

Coffee break . . .

 When we perceive a situation of threat or danger, this can lead to the psychological stress-response of anger. This is an emotional response that activates the fight/flight process.

 Stress *causes* anger and anger *causes* stress; there is a feed-back loop.

 You choose to be angry – it's your choice. Rephrase your internal self-talk or your dialogue to bring *control* back to you – or you will feel at the mercy of events.

 Your subjective view of 'reality' is different to everyone else's. Before you give in to an angry impulse try and see the situation from another person's point of view.

 Much of the time we're engaged in 'low level' anger – show-ing irritation, displeasure, annoyance. Anger in its extreme form is destructive and unhealthy – it triggers those undesirable chemicals from the brain and the stressed bodily sensations.

 Anger is an irrational response in these two instances: when there is *no* threat that needs to be dealt with; and when the level of anger is *inappropriate* to the situation that trig-gered it.

 Transient anger is usually activated by a situation and things calm down very quickly. With long-lasting anger the root cause is usually an unhealthy and 'distorted' way of thinking.

 Scientific research shows that anger differs from other un-healthy emotions in that there is a tendency to *not* want to let go of it.

When you *react* to feelings of anger you're out of control (reflex). When you *respond* to feelings of anger you're in control (thought).

 A change of thinking of the more rational 'Is it worth it?' or 'What do I want out of this?' type is often a better option.

Part

3

The 'past', 'present' and 'future' mind

Chapter

7

'First you forget names, then you forget faces. Next you forget to pull your zipper up and finally, you forget to pull it down.'

George Burns

Memory and the brain

How good is your memory? Do you appreciate how it defines you as a person?

You're probably fascinated by the fact that at times you can recall with great speed and accuracy things from long ago – and even things you never knew you knew! At other times you may wonder how it is that your memory lets you down when, for example, you walk into a room and forget why you went in there. Or when you forget a word that you've used maybe thousands of times. That pin number you've used time and time again. Your friend's telephone number. Or that universal favourite – forgetting names. In my experience, it is the number one 'complaint' I come across. Pretty much everyone cites this as a problem in everyday life.

This instance was recounted to me recently and is quite amusing. The perils of remembering (or in this case 'misremembering,' a name):

'Last week my wife and I went for dinner in a favourite local restaurant close by. One of our neighbours was there.

"Hi Phil, how's it going?" I said.

Then, while we were having our first course, I remembered his name was not Phil – it was in fact STEPHEN.

So now, all during the meal, I'm kicking myself for calling him Phil and I can't enjoy the food and I'm wondering what I could do.

Just as we'd finished dessert – which I couldn't taste because my mind was still on my embarrassment – I noticed Stephen walking towards the WC!

I rushed over to him while my wife settled the bill. I called him Stephen very loudly. I repeated it three more times in about a minute. The idea was to try and convince him that maybe he'd misheard me earlier on when I called him Phil.

Unfortunately, that's not the end of the story. When I woke up on Sunday morning, this name kept going through my head – 'SIMON, SIMON. His name is actually SIMON!'

(This is so typical of what happens in everyday life. What is it about names? What happened?)

'I just sort of remembered a name beginning with S that I could think of and the name Stephen came into my head!'

A moment's pause:

(John, while browsing magazines in the shop at the airport terminal, spots an ex-colleague and his wife.)

John: 'Ed – I don't believe it! How long's it been?'

Ed: 'Hey – John! How's it going? We're off to Paris for a few nights. Good deal on a suite at that lovely old hotel, the Millennium Opera. What about you?'

John: 'Yeah, wife and I are just nipping over to New York for a week. Talking about Paris, we were there last month. Had dinner twice at this fantastic restaurant we discovered over on the Left Bank. Run by a nice lady – a real find.'

Ed: 'We'll try it. What's it called?'

John: 'Erm – let me think. I'm good with names usually . . . err. What's that herb that you usually have with lamb?'

Ed: 'You mean . . . Rosemary?'

John: 'That's the one.' (*Then he calls out to his wife who's browsing the books.*) 'Rosemary, what's the name of that restaurant we discovered in Paris?'

How can we even begin to talk about the brain's importance? It stores our memories, our hopes, our dreams, our dislikes, our fears and our thoughts. We can't hope to understand its 'multitasking' role without taking a look at the body's whole nervous system – of which the brain forms one part; and the most important part. Its job is to interpret and store information from the senses and use this to control the body.

One thing that we do know about the brain (or mind) is that despite its not being a muscle, the more activity we subject it to, the stronger it becomes and the better able it is to serve us in times of need. After all, there are upwards of 10 billion neurons waiting to be mobilised into action. Since, unlike a muscle, our brain's capacity is not subject to a limit in its power, it needs constant stimulation and challenge in order to stop our mental capability from weakening over time. I hate to bring up the 'use it or lose it' explanation – but there it goes!

I know how, as a child, as I mentioned in the Introduction, the constant pushing of the boundaries strengthened certain areas of the brain (even though I – and the psychologists who 'interviewed' me at the time – weren't sure why). Being able to do advanced multiplication tables and calculations seemed to strengthen other areas of the brain. It seemed to strengthen mental capabilities in functions *other* than numbers. The neuron 'connections' obviously stimulated other areas of the brain to do with language, for example; and also music, names and faces.

All of this from what I called 'overusing' the brain at a young age when it was still growing. Using 'associations' to enable the brain to remember more. It was noticeable that if I eased off in challenging the brain to do more work, it took a while to get back to that level of mental fitness. Rather like a muscle that grows weaker from not having been used for a while. But, I'm pleased to say, the capabilities continued from childhood into adult life.

When I'm instructing people during memory training sessions, it's those same 'associations' that they're being asked to forge in their minds in order to create the neural pathways that will enable them to retrieve a memory; these being formed by the dendrites reaching through the synapses and creating a link to the memory.

We now know that the more we do something, the more deeply we forge the *pathway* in the brain. If you imagine that you were a hiker who, along with many others, continually takes a path in the forest, then you notice that it becomes easier and easier because of the wearing down of the undergrowth. So when you're trying to retrieve a memory it helps if there has been frequent and recent activity. The pathway stays clear.

You can see, equally, how habits form. We get used to thinking in a certain way and so when we want to change our thinking a whole new neural pathway has to be forged. We have a memory of a certain habit that has been reinforced time and time again. If the 'pleasure' area of the brain is involved – it's even harder to break.

Neuroscience explores the relationship between the mind and the brain, and with the advancement in technology for studying the brain, memory is receiving more attention as it is the core of our very existence. As we discussed elsewhere, it was ancient philosophers who stressed the importance of our thinking and how it shapes our perception. The Greek philosopher Plato (428–348 BC) was one of the first to come up with an expla-nation relating to the aspects of the human mind. He suggested that the mind was a non-physical entity and used the Greek word 'psyche' (meaning soul) to describe this invis-ible entity.

In the field of memory he and his fellow philosophers pio-neered memory improvement principles that are used to the present day. As Plato rightly observed:

> **'All knowledge is but remembrance.'**

Encoding–storage–retrieval

Since all the processes relating to our memory take place in the brain, we'll first take a look at its workings and how it stores memories. A knowledge of the different areas of the brain with their different functions gives us a greater understanding of our own thoughts and behaviour. How the nerve cells lay down memories and then 'fire' at the appropriate moment to produce our recall is nothing less than miraculous.

In their quest to discover more and more about the mind, cognitive psychologists were quick to suggest that like our machine-counterparts we translate information into a form that is familiar – the computer takes the program in a language that it can understand; humans take some sensory stimulus (more on sensory memory later) and give it some mental representation. So, in effect, what we do is to encode, store, retrieve and then manipulate information stored in memory.

The three elements of encoding, storage and retrieval form the basis of the human memory. A breakdown in one or more of these elements is the reason for any kind of memory *malfunction*. Let's put it into less formal language: for 'I can't remember her name' or 'What was that password number?' or 'When's her birthday?' – read 'I've got a terrible memory!'

All the various pieces of information we receive through our senses are stored in different parts of the brain. We'll consider these and also look at the three main areas that neuroscientists have identified as the key to laying down memories:

(E) Encoding – the taking in of information.

(S) Storage – the storing of information.

(R) Retrieval – recalling the information when needed.

Put simply, we need to get information into our system (encode) in the first instance, then the capability of storing it somewhere (storage) – then finally we need to be able to locate it and retrieve it (retrieval).

All these three elements interact with each other to enable us to have an efficient memory system. However, from this it will be clear to you that a breakdown in *any* of these three processes equals – no memory. Whichever method (or memory technique) you use to register a piece of information (E) determines what and how the information gets stored (S) and that will limit what can be retrieved (R).

Let's take the analogy which is often cited by neuroscientists when discussing memories. You have a list of items on your shopping list – a frequent memory device used by people everyday. Let's say you have to give this list to someone who is doing the shopping for you. For the shopping trip to be satisfactory you would first have to write down the items so that they were legible to the shopper. If the list were to get wet in the rain, the ink would end up smudging (liken this to impaired storage), making the words less identifiable and a struggle to read (retrieval). So you can see that retrieval – the end result and the purpose of storing memories – is harder when the handwriting is bad (an encoding–retrieval action) or if the writing is smudged (a storage–retrieval action).

So when you say to yourself that you wish your memory was better, or you hear people coming out with the same refrain, just consider what it is you're asking for. You're asking for: much better recall – or retrieval, to use the official term.

As I mentioned earlier, a breakdown in (E) or (S) means no memory; in other words, no retrieval. What's the reason for most memory deficiency? It's at the encoding stage. We don't pay *attention* to things. If we don't focus on what we're listening to or what we're seeing then the experience passes us by. Quite often it's because we may be trying to 'process' more than one thing at a time. Whilst a lot of people pride themselves on their 'perceived' capability of doing a hundred things (exaggeration!) at once, the simple fact is as follows.

All the scientific studies show that:

- just trying to do even two things at the same time results in a loss of concentration for both tasks and therefore faulty recall.

Of course today we are all encouraged or compelled, out of necessity, to engage in 'multitasking'. But be aware that as far as memory is concerned, the reason why your brain is not cooperative on certain occasions is that while it may have registered some experiences in its short-term (or working) memory, without concentration and full attention it never reaches the long-term memory stage. It's being asked to split its focus onto too many actions.

Remember this: multitasking is the enemy of memory.

We're in an age of mobile phones, BlackBerrys, iPods and the rest of media bombarding us and vying for our attention. How many people do you see 'handling' two or more tasks at once; or with their gaze and fingertips focused on their mobile phones as they check or answer an e-mail?

Somebody remarked to me recently: 'Before, when you went out to lunch with someone – a client or business colleague – the first question after sitting down for a few minutes was 'white or red?'. Now, she said: 'I'm sitting there for ages while they're looking down and fiddling with their BlackBerry. And it doesn't get that much better during the meal – I'm talking to them while they're looking down. There's no attention. I often feel like Princess Diana when she said: "... *there were three of us in this marriage ...".*'

So, just to recap: if there's no encoding, because of the *split focus* of the brain on more than one task – then there's nothing to store; nothing's gone into the frontal lobes. Imagine going to one of those ubiquitous 'self-storage' places that you see dotted around the country. You turn up there with a van – with nothing in it – get the keys for your storage unit and load nothing into it. When you go back there the following month to retrieve your (imaginary) furniture and other belongings that were 'stored' – you come back with nothing. The cupboard is bare.

It's a bit like that with memory. If you don't notice something because you didn't pay attention, then it doesn't get processed by the brain – there's no *neural activity*. So there's nothing to store. So therefore there's nothing to recall. Again, the cupboard is bare. Unless you consciously notice or hear something then you cannot set about the task of committing it to your consciousness. If information does reach the brain it looks for associations to help you remember when the time comes. But you have to do some work, in the first instance; you have to pay attention. If there's no attention then short-term memories (or working memories) can't move into long-term memory.

*Multitasking is
the enemy
of memory*

Samuel Johnson put it well when he said:

> **'The true art of memory is the art of attention.'**

The brain's physiology

Let's take a look at the brain and its physiology. A brief understanding of its processes in the **formation of memories** will help you understand how breakdowns occur and how you can increase your memory power in the future.

The brain is an information processing device and the *physiology* of the brain is of direct interest to memory researchers. Neuroscientists (who spend their time studying the brain) have made great strides in studying this 2 to 3lb mass and, coupled with the cognitive psychologists (who spend time studying the mind), we now have an interface of the two elements and you'll hear the term 'cognitive neuroscience'. (The role of cognitive neuroscientists is to delineate the connections between mind and brain.)

Using tools like brain-imaging techniques we're able to see our cognitive 'processing' and its relation to brain function and structure. This enables us to obtain a lot of information about what is happening in the brain when we perform various activities such as remembering.

The nineties were dubbed 'the decade of the brain' as significant advances were made in the study of its anatomy, wonders and limitations. My observations are grounded in the latest neuroscience research that has been revolutionised through the use of the newer brain-imaging scans. These advances in technology have allowed scientists to observe the brain in action.

Advances in neuroscience have now proved that the brain is quite 'plastic' and is constantly being modified by our experiences.

You probably know quite a bit about the brain's structure already, in which case you'll know that we're talking about something that's:

- 2 to 3lb in weight (ever picked up a 2lb bag of sugar in the supermarket – heavy?);

- it is divided into two halves (we refer to them as the left and right hemispheres).

These are important distinctions. Being the centre of information processing, it would be helpful if we could identify where in the brain certain activity takes place; and that's exactly what cognitive neuroscientists have been able to tell us.

This is due to the imaging capabilities of machines such as electroencephalograms (EEGs), positron emission topography (PET scans) and functional magnetic resonance imaging (fMRI) that provide activity data for the entire brain or specific regions.

Essentially the brain is a collection of nerve cells or neurons (as we saw in Chapter 1). Forming part of our central nervous system (CNS), these brain cells communicate with other cells individually or as part of a network of millions or billions of other cells. Awe-inspiring figures, but then we're looking at an organ that has billions of neurons and trillions of connections at the synapses (more about that in a moment).

Although the brain is often likened to a computer, to appreciate its capabilities we have to remember that it is a biological organ that grows and evolves. During all of our waking hours – and even during sleep – we're engaging in experiences that create a network of neural 'pathways' that are essential in forging retrievable memories. In order to execute their complex tasks, all of the neurons have to communicate back and forth with each other by twin processes that are:

1 **Electrical**: via the nerve impulses.

2 **Chemical**: using neurotransmitters.

A neuron looks a little like a small plant with a root at both ends.

From the body of the neuron there are hundreds of threads known as dendrites; these have the task of *picking up signals* from neighbouring cells.

Then there is the long stem called the axon; the part of the individual neuron that *passes on signals* to other neurons.

Communication between the neurons is at the synapse; the *junction* between communicating cells.

A nerve impulse travels down the axon to the terminal junction and then crosses the synaptic cleft using brain chemicals called neurotransmitters. The two neurons *never actually make contact* as the impulse is taken across the gap by the neurotransmitters.

Where are these brain chemicals (the neurotransmitters) stored, you might ask? Handily, they are in the nerve endings in tiny sacs that are known as vesicles. When the signal reaches the nerve ending the contents of the sac floods the gap and *bind* to the receptor sites of the nearby cell.

Cells that fire together wire together

Exciting developments over the last two decades or so have shown that the synapses are continually adapting and changing and we now have the term 'neuroplasticity' to describe this. Our brains are plastic and the synapses are altering each time we encode a memory. So we're constantly rewiring our brains. We make connections with other neurons and so if we associate an image, for example, with something we want to remember, the neurons will fire together to make that connection. You may have heard the phrase 'cells that fire together wire together'.

The connections for our memories get *stronger* the more we use them. This can be just recalling the words of a song or, equally, practising a backhand volley. You *weaken* the connections through lack of use and strengthen them with increased usage. How many times have you heard the phrase 'use it or lose it' when applied to the brain?

What has been even more fascinating in the discovery of neuroplasticity is that just *thinking* about or carrying out specific actions in your mind changes its structure. So practising with the strings of a guitar in your head actually *rewires* your brain! This makes it easier when you get round to actually practising as you've strengthened those areas of the brain. **This has an important bearing on visualising outcomes in various situations** (see Chapter 8).

The cerebral cortex

The outer layer and wrinkled area with which we are all familiar is known as the cerebral cortext. This is the primary place that all the higher cognitive functions like *communicating* and *remembering* happen. Just beneath it there is an essential and complex structure that is involved with *emotion* and *memory*, forming part of the limbic system.

Let's talk more about this cerebral cortex, that we know is comprised of two hemispheres. Separating the two is a deep groove that is comprised of a bundled network of nerves called the corpus callosum that are each divided into four major areas termed lobes, each responsible for different functions.

Immediately behind the forehead is the frontal lobe that stretches to around the middle of the top of your head. In the posterior area of this lobe is the motor cortex, responsible for voluntary movements and the front area, or prefrontal cortex, responsible for higher motor control. In this area also resides a portion – known as Broca's area – devoted to the physical production of speech.

Just to the rear of the frontal lobe (roughly under the crown of your head) is the parietal (middle) lobe, where the somatosensory cortex area lies. It is here that bodily sensations such as touch, temperature and pain are formulated. With respect to cognitive processes, the parietal lobe also is responsible for – amongst other things – regulating the processes of working memory and attention. This area processes spatial information and is responsible for creating mental images and recognising people's faces.

Just below the parietal lobe is the occipital lobe that contains the primary visual cortex – the area of the brain responsible for vision and the ability to recognise visual patterns. The optic nerve ends in this area and these lobes process information into colour, shape and objects.

The fourth and final lobes are the temporal (side) lobes located just behind the ears. The auditory cortex is here, the primary sensory area for hearing and sense of balance. They also include Wernicke's area, responsible for speech comprehension. Language is an important function for the temporal lobes and they are also responsible for the all-important *transfer of short-term memories to long-term memory*.

There are many areas of the cortex that are not specifically allied to any motor or sensory function. Neuroscientists have called these *association* areas of the cortex. They believe that these are responsible for integrating the processing of other functions of the brain, such as language processing, problem solving and decision-making.

Because of these 'unused' parts, you constantly hear claims that we only use 2% or 10% of our brains (depending on the article), the theory being that these association areas – that perform no specific function – are lying dormant, waiting for something to do! They are necessary for *integrating* – rather like a symphony – information from all the other different brain areas.

The two hemispheres of the cortex – the right and left – have different functions. You may already know that the left side actually receives information from the right side of the body and also controls its movements; likewise the right side of the brain controls – and receives information from – the left side of the body. This is known as the principle of *contralaterality* – each of the two brain hemispheres are responsible for controlling the functions of the **opposite** side of the body.

You're probably familiar with the 'shorthand' descriptions of left brain and right brain functions (we'll cover that below with male and female differences). It's in the area of verbal ability that the differences are pronounced, with the left hemisphere being responsible for verbal processing and the right being relatively nonverbal. Continuing research shows that the left side is primarily involved in language processing.

Our right side seems to be specialised in the performance of spatially related activities. It's important to remember that rather than each side having clear-cut tasks, the two areas work *together* in close interaction as part of an integrated system.

Any differences in the male and female brain?

If you looked at the male and female brain you'd see that the male brain is around 10% larger than the female's even after taking body size into account. This doesn't mean that the mental processing capacity of females is any less because of that. The number of brain cells is the same. It just means that they are spread more densely in the woman's brain.

In the past this was a delicate area to talk about – the phrase 'gender stereotypes' was bandied around – and studies were halted because of the sensitivity of the subject. Now, with the leaps and bounds in the area of brain science, we can see how and why the male and female mind *process* information differently. Same computer – different software.

Interesting research by Dr L. Brizendine (University of California, San Francisco Medical School) as to the influence of chemistry and *hormones* on women's brain states – and therefore moods – showed how the effects of these were responsible for creating a woman's *reality* from day to day. Her findings revealed that this was responsible for a woman's values and preferences almost from day one, and the consequent thought processes and behaviour through every stage of life.

Her research showed that each stage introduces new hormonal states, stretching from childhood to adolescence to early adulthood to potential motherhood, right up to menopause. The conclusion therefore for the differences in the minds of men and women? Due to fluctuations starting in the first months of life and progressing until post-menopause: '*a woman's neurological reality is not as constant as a man's.*'

- 'His is like a mountain that is worn away imperceptibly over the millennia by glaciers, weather . . .'
- 'Hers is more like the weather itself – constantly changing and hard to predict.'

Women's 'sixth sense' or intuition

Research in neuroscience has thrown up some interesting facts about the male and female brain. The two hemispheres – left and right – are constantly at work together in everything in which we engage. Naturally, that's the same for both males and females. What has been discovered is that the corpus callosum (mentioned earlier; and see Figure 7.1), the thick band of fibres that connect both of the hemispheres – is denser for women than it is for men. You'll remember that these fibres connect the neurons that are firing from the two different sides of the brain. So women have better connectivity between the two parts of the brain.

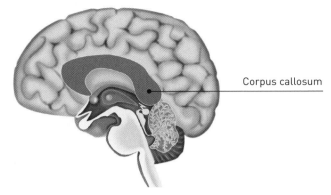

Corpus callosum

Figure 7.1 The corpus callosum

Some interesting findings relating to women and the process-ing of language have gradually been emerging. We know that women have more neurons in the left side of the brain com-pared to men. This is the side of the brain concerned with language and memory skills.

Women tend to perform better than men in tests connected with verbal learning. In addition, women have a higher concen-tration of dopamine in this part of the brain. So in listening and speaking women have been found to use more of their brains than men do. There was an interesting study conducted by J. Lurito and M. Phillips in the USA at the Indiana University School of Medicine (2000) when an extract of a John Grisham novel was read out to a male and female audience. When 'pro-cessing' sentences (as opposed to single words) men use just a specific area of the brain on the left side and women use the same area but on *both* sides of the brain (just above the ears).

What this means is that the left and right sides of a woman's brain tend to perform more evenly when they're communicat-ing with each other. How does that manifest itself in everyday life? Well, the left side of the brain is responsible for detail and language, as we've just discussed. The right side is concerned with visual and spatial information; and just as the left is biased towards detail, the right is biased towards the 'big picture'.

The right hemisphere communicates more with the areas of the brain that lie below the cortex and so is more concerned with *emotion* than the 'logical' and linear left hemisphere. So the right area of the brain is more attuned to emotion and since women have a better *connection* between the two sides – they are perceived to be more *intuitive* than men. Emotional memories tend to be encoded better in the brain. So it may be that some women – apart from their intuitiveness – have better memory skills because of the way in which the information is stored. It's often been said:

> **Men *forget* but never forgive.**
> **Women *forgive* but never forget.**

So if you thought women's intuition (or that '*sixth sense*') was a myth, maybe it's time to revise your thinking. We know that in the female brain there is a much higher density of nerve cells in the lobe that is concerned with language – the temporal lobe. This language advantage, along with the 'connection' differential, may account for why most women display more empathy and generally pick up the emotional cues from spoken words better than men.

Memories and the limbic system

Just beneath the cerebral cortex is a complex system of structures known as the limbic system.

This area plays a vital part in **learning** and **remembering** information and also the processing of **emotion**. It has five main elements:

- **hippocampus** – is vital for ENCODING new information into memory.

- **amygdala** – has a key role in regulating emotions and in forming emotional memories.

- **thalamus** – serves primarily as a relay point that routes incoming sensory information to the appropriate area of the brain (visual to visual cortex, and so on) and also seems to play a role in attention.

- **hypothalamus** – just below the thalamus; controls the body's hormones (endocrine system) and plays an important role in emotions.

- **basal ganglia** – critical role in controlling movement and important for motor-based memories, such as riding a bike.

It can't be stressed enough: whilst there are *specific* areas and structures of the brain responsible for certain functions like memory, there is a symphony of interconnections between the various areas and structures such that we're looking at the *co-ordinated* action of many regions. Our memory function is dispersed through different areas of the brain.

Let's look at the amygdala, which we've covered in earlier chapters relating to our 'tortured' mind. This section is a specialist in remembering emotionally laden positive or negative events. As such it is responsible for our fearful memories. And it's tough to shift them!

Remember the feel of a spider on your skin? Do you jump – even when it's not a spider? The amygdala notifies us of impending danger. The trouble is, as you've seen, it operates at an elevated level during periods of stress and anxiety. The cortisol released during stressed or anxious moments is not good for the heart – and it's also very damaging to the brain, especially the hippocampus (more on that below).

You may remember that the hippocampus is the centre for learning and memory. Cortisol ultimately destroys some of the cells in the hippocampus and prevents the formation of new neurons. This results in shrinkage and consequently affects our learning and memory. In addition, cortisol leads to poor memory retrieval when you're in momentary stressful encounters. Do you notice your mind going blank when you're in an uncomfortable situation? Have you forgotten information that's well known to you in the heat of a stressful moment? It's not your fault – it's the cortisol. **And of course, the more stressed or worried you get in a situation, the more of the chemical is dispensed and the worse your thinking.** You can see why deep breathing, counting to ten (or higher!) or any other relaxation response, will pay dividends at these times.

The hippocampus, however, has been identified as a key player in the formation and retrieval of memories. It is the only area of the brain that has been found to be able to produce new neurons. Neuroscientists have therefore been promoting the benefits of physical and also mental exercise as it has been shown to lead to parts of the brain working together in the cerebral cortex which links to the hippocampus. As these paths are repeatedly crossed the 'sheath' of *myelin* thickens which enables more accurate and quicker recall. Repetition is the key.

Psychologists seek answers to the same questions relating to the mind as did *philosophers* before them. Now we have mechanisms to test real world behaviour rather than relying on abstract theories. Some argue that by understanding the brain we can understand the mind. There are also those that say that the two should be studied *separately*.

The argument centres on the fact that:

- the brain is a *physical* entity;
- while the mind is an *abstract* concept (that many believe is equivalent to a soul).

The best way to appreciate the two elements is to use a computer analogy by regarding:

> **The brain as the *hardware*.**
> **The mind as the *software*.**

The information processing brain

In order to appreciate this 'mind power' that we all have, it's worth looking at the development of the computer, which introduced to society the existence of a machine that could 'think' for us in certain ways.

A machine that was able to be programmed so that it could carry out functions that were once thought possible only by the intelligent human mind. The way that a computer functions was soon seized upon as a metaphor for describing the mental or cognitive processing that occurs in the human memory.

In other words, how – like a computer – we process 'data' in the first instance and then store, retrieve and use it. We have a short-term memory – rather like a computer's RAM application – which we need to store information for the moment but which we don't need to 'save'. Then we have our long-term memory which is 'saved' on the hard disk.

Scientists a few decades ago found it handy to offer the concept of the brain as hardware and the mind as software. We know that energy is needed by the brain in order to function well; it needs 'software' to process information and when the brain is turned 'off' like a machine, the software cannot run. There's one area, though, that has been updated over the last 20 years or so. It was thought that 'thinking' in the brain was purely an electrical activity and therefore we were bound by our inherited 'hardware' – reinforcing the computer analogy. However, we now know that the *chemical* activity is immense and has changed the idea of our limitations.

It's easy to draw analogies between the way that the brain stores and retrieves information and the way that a computer does. When we store memories it is the result of electrochemical activity that changes the physical structure of our brain – and we use the same electrochemical process to retrieve that memory. As we saw earlier on, the network of neurons literally represents the memory itself.

We looked at the importance of the thalamus and the hippocampus in memory consolidation. When we create short-term memories with the resulting interaction of different neurons 'talking to each other', it leaves a 'trace' behind – imagine footsteps in the snow. Do you get the idea?

The more we bring up the memory the easier it is for the neurons to 'fire' and the easier will be the recall. Supplying the mind with an appropriate association brings back the long-term memory.

Impressive though computers are, however, we should remember the power of the human brain. There are some things that are in our favour, so computers may not quite take over the world.

- We can lose some data (or all of it) from a fault in the disk or another part of the machine.

The magnificence of the human brain means that our memories are stored in different parts and are triggered by 'associations'. So if we lose a link (from a brain impairment) we can recover a memory by locating an alternative route (neural pathway) to the desired information.

- The computer can only take specific information and store it as it is (you're familiar with the phrase 'Garbage In Garbage Out – GIGO).

We take information in and using our pre-existing knowledge and intuition we then store it – after we have assigned 'meaning' to it. So we can be more selective in what is stored in the memory and of course that means we are more flexible in the information that can be stored.

Of course we are capable of GIGO in one sense. That's the whole principle of 'distorted' thinking.

We may interpret things in a certain way and store memories based on that *faulty* thinking. So the conversations we have with ourselves are based on those unhelpful thoughts of the past.

(Hopefully, with the *MindControl* model, you're able to challenge those memories now.)

We have to envy the memory capability of the computer:

● The transfer of data from the screen (the working memory) to the longer-term memory of the hard disk is achieved in an instant with a keystroke.

Despite the wonders of the brain, our transfer from short-term (or working) memory to long-term memory is not so smooth. It's a continual process of 'strengthening' *connections* between neurons. We also have to work hard at an accurate memory transfer as, unlike machines, we store memories through a network of associations. And of course when we're talking about our own memory the information that we encode, store, retrieve (ESR) is naturally subjective and is influenced by our 'state' at the time as well as other factors.

Episodic memory and semantic memory

When was it you last went to the theatre? Where were you when you heard the result of the election? Which way does the Queen's head face on a £1 coin? In which country is the Eiffel Tower?

The answers to these questions come from the two elements of memory – **episodic memory** and **semantic memory** – that come under the umbrella of *explicit memory*.

Semantic memory is your knowledge about the world in general and the names of things and how to identify them. If I told you I had just bought an iPod that would become part of your semantic memory – of course you may forget this the next day or before. If you're introduced to somebody whose name is Francesca then this becomes part of your semantic memory (and also your *episodic* – we'll discuss that later) – but you may forget her name five minutes later. The name of the current prime minister – that's semantic memory. Recognise that picture of Marilyn Monroe – that's semantic memory. If you know that the hunk of metal with four wheels is called a car – and recognise it as such – that's semantic memory. Going through the revolving doors into an office building and pressing the button for the lift – that's semantic memory. The colour of the iconic London Routemaster bus? The colour of a carrot? The taste of mint? The taste of gin? All semantic memory.

These are all examples of semantic memory. You can see how important it is in your everyday life. We all possess a vast store of this type of memory. Apart from our personal lives there is always a huge amount of semantic memory related to your working life. You'll have specific knowledge – compared to the next person – relating just to your specialised area. As well as that you'll know things relating to your hobbies and interests that other people will not.

Closely allied to this memory is episodic memory, which is related to your memory of events that occurred at a specific time at a specific location. There is often an overlap between the two memories since they are the two most important types of memory relating to our 'conscious' awareness. For example, if you remember meeting your girlfriend for lunch at a sushi bar last week, then this is an example of episodic memory. Also, there was a huge element of semantic memory related to that afternoon's encounter.

First, things about her. You remembered her face – a great help. Saved you ending up having lunch with – and footing the bill for – *a complete stranger!* You also remembered her name – saved you from embarrassment (if you'd called her Vanessa instead of Emma)!

As far as the venue was concerned, you knew where it was, how to take the dishes off the conveyor belt and the methods of eating the various dishes. And you also possessed some general knowledge of how to pay by credit card with the machine at the end. All examples of semantic memory related to this episodic event. So although the two types of memory are connected they are distinctly different. When you retrieve information from the semantic memory it is not related to the past and your experiences in the way that the episodic memory is related.

There have been some interesting findings that show the difference between the two types and how the brain processes the information for the relevant memories. In one review of nearly 150 patients who were suffering from amnesia, there was an impairment of their episodic memory in *all* cases and, in contrast, many had only modest deficiencies in their semantic memory. So the effects of brain damage were more connected with episodic memory than semantic.

In other findings, this time relating to retrograde amnesia (an impaired retention of information acquired *before* the onset of amnesia), patients displayed much worse performance relating to episodic memory, not being able to recall personal experiences prior to the brain damage (as shown in the film *The Bourne Identity*). The semantic knowledge acquired prior to an accident was unaffected in nearly all of the cases, giving strong backing to the evidence that the two types of memory are quite distinct.

With the development of brain imaging machines, further proof has been acquired showing that the memories are separate. While being scanned, in 20 studies, participants were asked to perform various tasks in connection with memory. The premise of the studies was this: if semantic and episodic are distinct and *different* then – in the imaging machines – *different* areas of the brain would light up during learning (encoding) and retrieval.

It was found that in the 20 brain imaging studies connected with learning (*encoding*), the following happened:

- the left prefrontal cortex was more active during episodic than semantic encoding in 18 of them.

In 26 brain imaging studies connected with *retrieval*:

- the right prefrontal cortex was more active during episodic memory retrieval than semantic retrieval in 25 of the cases.

'The name's . . .'

This is an interesting scenario recounted to me – in one form or another – by many people on the subject of names and their importance to us that highlights our natural instinct to remember and get names right!

Autobiographical memory

We'll look at an important aspect of semantic and episodic memory now: autobiographical memory. Memories that we have relating to ourselves and our interactions with the world, spanning a period of time. When we remember things about ourselves – childhood, schools, where we live, work, play – these are autobiographical and also a part of our own *personal* semantic memory. Yet these memories are probably the most important to us.

They play an important role in determining our self-esteem or self-worth. Remembering good things that you did or that happened to you are essential mood-enhancers when you're feeling bad. We've seen earlier how faulty thinking sets off a chain of negative emotions. Unless they're disputed with logical questions – often relating to your past experiences and how you coped and how you felt – then the irrational beliefs and thoughts take over. Neuroscientists talk of **mood-congruent** memory – how negative recollections are summoned to the mind when we're feeling down (as we've seen in previous chapters) instead of positive and upbeat memories.

We tend to store these memories as our life story (to date) – based around the usual themes of childhood, adolescence, student days, work, relationships – all with specific *episodic* memories.

Sometimes these memories are stored inaccurately: 'data' that, at the time, was based on our *opinions* – not facts.

Of course if we keep dredging up autobiographical facts that were based on our 'distorted' thinking at the time, we do nothing to change our lives for the better. The Canadian psychologist Endel Tulving (1972) proposed the distinction between episodic and semantic memory that has been used since then. He also introduced the concept of 'mental time travel'.

Tulving was referring to the fact that the brain allows us to re-experience some aspect of the original episode; it allows us to visit a memory and 'relive' the events and to use that information for the future.

That means we have the capability to reassess a memory and change our *attitude – if* it was based on unhealthy and inaccurate thinking at the time. This means we can change our present feelings.

> **Remember: it's never too late to**
> **change a memory.**

We may remember sensory detail for many of these instances, depending on the emotional intensity or attachment to the events. The thunderstorm during your driving test. The expression on the face of your head teacher – 30 years ago – when she told you of the award you had won. The stark meeting room in which you had your first job interview. It is often the 'sensory' detail that provides us with good recall of distant memories. The information picked up by our senses also confirms that our recollections are broadly accurate and, more importantly, genuine.

Our recollections of these sensory-enhanced memories are usually visual. When we are extremely moved by something or experience emotional intensity or shock, the visual memory remains strong and this is why we may recollect disturbing memories as 'flashbacks'.

It's never too late to change a memory

Coffee break . . .

 Despite the brain not being a muscle, the more activity to which we subject it the **stronger** it becomes. (Unlike a muscle our brain's capacity is not subject to a limit in its power.)

 Memories are strengthened through 'associations' that forge new neural pathways to aid retrieval.

 How important is memory? Memory is everything – *'all knowledge is but remembrance'*.

 There are three elements that are essential in the formation of memories: encoding, storage, retrieval. A breakdown in any one of them causes problems.

 The reason for most of our memory deficiency? It's at the encoding stage – mainly because we don't pay *attention*.

 Advances in neuroscience now show that the brain is 'plastic' and is modified by our experiences. We are constantly 'rewiring' our brain.

 Memories are forged in the brain by the neurons engaging in electrical (via nerve impulses) and chemical (using neurotransmitters) activity.

 The hippocampus and the amygdala (in the limbic system) play a vital part in learning and remembering information and the storing of 'emotional' memories.

 Our memories are stored in *different* parts of the brain and are triggered by associations.

Research shows that the male and female brain process information *differently* in some instances. Women have better connectivity between the two parts (left and right) of the brain.

 Semantic and episodic memory are the two primary elements of memory that cause us difficulty in everyday life. Using mnemonics can help us to some extent (as can paying more attention).

Chapter

8

'A champion is afraid of losing.
Everyone else is afraid of winning.'

Billie Jean King

The 'winner' takes it all

It will be obvious to you by now that being able to take charge of the mind is very much a skill. The 'winners' in life are those of us who learn to win control of and use the mind so that it serves us. Not the other way round. Our unhelpful thoughts may tell us that we don't deserve success. It may be a long-standing belief that stems from childhood or events that have knocked your self-esteem. If you don't think, deep down, that you're worthy of success – you'll make sure that you lose.

As I said way back in the early chapters, and it bears repeating multiple times: the mind is given to you. You are not given to the mind. The power to change your thinking and attract more success in your life is not so much as in your own hands – *it's in your own head*. The game of life is bestowed upon us. How much we choose to participate and effect positive outcomes is usually a function of how much we are able to overpower our fears and negative thought process.

It's not an exaggeration to say that most people spend their time *not* pursuing what they really want out of life – their goals and dreams – and become quite expert at it. Then they spend the rest of the time beating themselves up over their failures and lost opportunities with all the 'I should have . . .' and 'I could have . . .' statements and other forms of distorted thinking. All the success in life that we experience is the result of our thoughts – as is all the failure, too.

A lot of the time we use the power of our internal dialogue to talk us out of doing something because we're focused on failure of some sort. If we had a friend or relative who spent much of the time criticising us and our circumstances we wouldn't put up with it. Yet we'll listen to the repetitive self-limiting and critical statements of our self-talk.

What about those people that you've met over the years that may have had a dream or a vision about something?

'One day you'll see my name up in lights on Broadway.'

'I'm going to be a lawyer and help people.'

'I'll have a red Ferrari after I've qualified and made a success of myself.'

'We're going to get our house built one day and we'll have those ornamental gates.'

'I'll never amount to anything in life.'

'I'm not cut out for office type work. I'll probably just end up doing menial jobs.'

'It's not worth going for that . . . there's too much competition.'

'I'll stick to what I know . . . doesn't pay much but I've been doing it for 15 years now.'

Well, the first four probably may have achieved a self-fulfilling optimistic outcome (even if they didn't achieve the actual dream or goal) and probably the bottom four as well! Those people with an optimistic outlook are the ones who say: 'One day . . .' or 'I'm going to . . .' and work towards something and do whatever is in their power to try and make it come true. All through the power of thought and imagery. Equally, the self-fulfilling prophecy applies to the bottom four statements as well – through the same power of thought and imagery.

Optimism and pessimism are powerful forces. We've all come to realise through our experiences that our own personal expectations of success or failure can influence what happens to us in life. We create a 'ripple effect' through our optimism and pessimism. If we expect something good to happen our mind is on constant 'lookout' for *serendipitous* opportunities that may come our way and influence a successful outcome (the person with a pessimistic tendency would be 'blind' to this). 'Pessimism', just for your interest, is derived from the Latin *pessimus* meaning 'worst'). If we expect a negative outcome our mind, with its thought–feeling–behaviour mechanism which you now know so well, makes sure that we're led down the path to that outcome.

It's interesting to note that researchers studying the twin areas of optimism and pessimism discovered some interesting things in terms of expectations. They found that optimists believe and expect favourable things will happen as opposed to '*hoping*' that things will turn out this way. In the case of the pessimists surveyed, they tend to expect a poor outcome.

I mentioned earlier my chance encounter with some words relating to optimism and pessimism and how it seemed to me that there was really only one path to go down. Certainly, the continued research into this area shows strongly that whichever way you measure the findings on optimism, there is nearly always:

- happiness
- achievement of goals/dreams
- perseverance
- good health.

With pessimism there is often a link to:

- unhappiness
- reluctance to cope with 'problems'
- poor health
- 'blaming' tendency.

An intensive research study by C.S. Carver and M.F. Scheier (1981), experts in the two areas, noted that some people could be termed as having 'dispositional' optimism about life in general. They maintain that state pretty much most of the time. Others may have optimism about specific situations.

Central to this finding is that 'attitude', which is a specific way of thinking and therefore feeling, is crucial as it determines whether you feel positive or negative about certain things. Furthermore, attitudes are learned. We know from everything that we've discussed so far that anyone can achieve more in life by changing their negative way of thinking – we're not as helpless in this game of life as many people prefer to believe.

We've spent a lot of time in raising awareness of the fact that most of our thoughts are of a negative nature. In addition, we've explored how all thoughts, good or bad, have a direct influence on how we *feel* from moment to moment and how we *behave*. We have good thoughts, bad thoughts, self-limiting thoughts, and confident thoughts. Everything in life that you like is from thought; equally everything that you hate is from thought.

We hear about waste all the time. Governments talk about waste in their manifestos and how they'll clamp down on this, that and the other. Local councils do the same. Yet the biggest waste is what we don't do in life. Until we change our thinking we are stuck in the same rut and never leave the starting block.

> **The thing we waste most of in our lives – *is our life*.**

Images are everything

What is often taken for granted or overlooked by many of us is the *way* that we think. That is to say, how it is usually manifested. It tends to be through *images*.

Consider how you bring back memories from the past, including those formative years of childhood. It's usually pictures and images flashing by in a mini-movie, perhaps along with some sounds or even smells. These memories are not evoked by words, it's all imagery.

What do you do when you're hearing a play on the radio? What colour is your car? Can you think of your kitchen right now?

What about the worktop – is there an electric kettle on it? And the refrigerator – open the door; what can you see on the shelves? What about the power of a favourite song to transport you back to a time that you remember well? What chain of images did that one song produce in your mind? What about a beach, blue sky and golden sand – can you conjure up that in your mind?

You've just been using your imagination to create pictures – to visualise. The mind is expert at doing this. It's totally natural. Similarly, if somebody recounts a story of a mishap or pleasant experience to us we'll start creating – through the imagination – a sequence of images that gives us meaning about the event. Our imaginations are very powerful. We saw how the power of distorted thinking – which is pure imagination coupled with imagery – can misinterpret events and hold us back from achieving goals.

> **If we learn to use our imagination in a guided way it can propel us to success in all areas of life.**

Even Albert Einstein was minded to comment on imagination with his famous utterance: '*Imagination is more important than knowledge.*'

Visualise to realise

The power of imagery is the essence of visualisation. You may have heard this word in connection with sportspeople and some business leaders. If you are familiar with this term it's because it is a highly effective way of using mind power to become a 'winner' – in all aspects of life. Essentially it's about visualising outcomes.

We can use visualisation for any situation. We're used to doing it every day – unconsciously. It's as easy as breathing. Set up a blank screen in your mind. You make instances become more real. It makes you devote attention to something – **a precursor**

for action – so you're more likely to achieve your goals and dreams. And what is a visualisation similar to, anyway? A dream.

Because we think in images, visualisation is an easy process to master. Just consider for a moment everything we've looked at from the beginning of the book. We know that we make 'internal representations' in our head as we play out conversations and 'produce' and 'direct' 'mini movies'.

Since we give so much credence to the sounds and images in our mind it means that – with our highly capable imagination – we're very proficient at producing a soundtrack and pictures of things going wrong. Do you agree?

So how about a movie with things going right?

And it gives you confidence in whatever discipline in which you're trying to be successful. We know that people who use the visualisation process will picture a scenario and go right through the process visually to a successful outcome. They'll 'build in' any complications that could arise – and deal with them, in their head. When it comes to actually doing the 'task', the fact that we've engaged in 'mental time travel' (remember that from the last chapter?) into the future means that we've anticipated how to sort out and deal with any possible complications. This increases our chance of achieving what we want.

For example (and this is quite a common one), you have been selected to give a talk for 20 minutes to an assembled audience of 200 people at an upcoming ball. How would visualisation work for this?

There are two ways of handling it:

1 You can go through the **whole** process:
   (a) You could imagine yourself walking up to the stage to applause.
   (b) You could be talking confidently to an enraptured audience.

(c) Answering questions in the Q&A session confidently.

(d) Being thanked at the end by the MC.

(e) Leaving to the sound of applause.

I was going to add, watching your car being towed away by the clampers as you walk to hotel reception – but that's being cruel! Delete. (You can do that with visualisation, you see.)

2 You can just focus on the **end** result:

(a) You could have the picture of the MC thanking you for a great session as they shake your hand amidst the sound of rapturous applause from the assembled audience.

(b) You leave and give a wave to the delighted audience.

If, for example, you were a little concerned about the Q&A before the event then it helps to go through the process in which you confidently enact handling the session.

The reason why visualisation is so powerful and so effective is because we know that the imagining is *creating* neural pathways of experience even though we haven't physically enacted the 'event'. Neuroscience, as noted earlier, has shown us that our thoughts actually alter the brain's wiring and its biochemistry. This gives familiarity to the episode. *So it's as though we've already been there before.* And of course we so often experience the feeling of 'threat' in a new and unfamiliar situation. This gives the illusion of the experience *and* an end result. You've set up a 'blueprint'. So instead of having unhelpful images of uncertainty – as we typically do in a new and stressful situation – we have positive images for the mind to work on. And like attracts like.

Sportspeople make extensive use of training the neural pathways in the brain by the use of visualisation, as it is a very important part of the science of sports psychology. The subconscious mind is fertile ground for them.

Just as in the example above, the sportsperson has the experience of achieving the goal and how they feel when they achieve it. And they've been on the track, in the swimming pool, football field or tennis court already. They use all of their senses – in addition to the visual – as they hear (auditory) the crowd and feel the vitality in their body (kinaesthetic). Just like real-live practice, they can repeatedly experience the 100m race or toss the ball up and hit the second serve ace on match point at Wimbledon. This gives the illusion of having been in a pressure situation and coming through it. It encourages belief and promotes that mental toughness that we keep hearing about in the world of sport. As sportspeople strengthen the path for the neurons in the brain through constant repetition, they become more proficient once they are in the actual situation or in practice.

Jonny Wilkinson, England's record-points scorer in international rugby, illustrated the power of visualisation very well when he said: '*I cannot overestimate how much controlling the mind is crucial to my life as a goal-kicker in rugby union. You have to be able to see perfection before you can achieve it. So I might do parts of a practice session in which I set up a ball, go through the motions, see the kick in my head . . . that can be a perfect session . . .*'*

The power of the mind was evident on 6 May 1954 when athletic history was made on a track at Oxford University as Britain's Roger Bannister achieved what was thought impossible. Running a mile in four minutes. He broke the world record in achieving a time of 3:59:4.

Many others had been trying to achieve the four or sub-four minute mile for years. Bannister's secret was to split his training sessions into doing four laps of the track and aiming to do each one in a minute or below. (How often have you been told to break down a task in your mind into manageable chunks?)

*© *The Times* and 4th Feb 2010/nisyndication.com

Roger Bannister

When the 'holy grail' had been achieved it was not too long before other hopefuls broke that record. Just 46 days later one of his greatest rivals (with a previous best of 4:02) lowered the figure to 3:58. Four years later 3:54 was achieved. The figure has been lowered time and time again over the last half-century. Bannister's inspiration to others was obvious: **you can if you think you can**. He believed in himself and his ability to achieve the dream.

Bannister always stressed the importance of the power of the mind in winning or losing. He believed in himself and his ability to break the record. He once said that apart from the obvious physiology, *'psychology and other factors set the razor's edge of defeat or victory'*.

Nowhere is the use of visualisation as prevalent as in the game of tennis. Essentially a 'mind game' where important points are won or lost in the flicker of a neuron. In a game with a scoring system in which there are literally so many 'pressure points', a whole match can run away from you with just one bad point. Mental toughness is key in this sport. Powerful self-talk and powerful imagery. The consistent champions who emerge now and again are the ones that have that 'X factor' and play the 'big' points well during the pressurised situation. Time and again you'll see champions like Roger Federer and Rafael Nadal get out of tight situations not just because of their timely ground strokes, but because of their determination and mental training.

Roger Federer and Rafael Nadal

Many of you may have seen or remember reading or hearing about a breathtaking example of the power of the mind, in a historic first round tennis match played in the first week of Wimbledon – in June 2010 – between John Isner and Nicolas Mahut. A match that captivated even non-sporting audiences as news bulletins were rejigged all around the world to report on this: *the longest match in tennis history.*

Both players consistently 'held serve' in the fifth and final set and the game was locked at a mind-boggling 59–59 when poor light stopped play, after more than seven hours. Play resumed the next day and again each player held serve – under extreme mental pressure – and it became more of who was going to 'crack' first, rather than who was going to be the winner. Most people could not think of anyone being a loser in this match as the outcome would be decided by just a single game; and in tennis that can be just a single *point*. John Isner was the fortunate player on the day as at 69–68 he was able to benefit from his opponent's one wayward shot that handed him 'game, *sweat* and match!' – 70–68 – after a total match time of a staggering 11 hours. They were both physically drained but their sheer determination and mental resilience carried them through.

Many successful people in life change their thinking by adopting the process of visualisation to see their goals and dreams already fulfilled. By making a situation seem more like 'reality' it sheds the distorted thinking process and encourages action. So they put themselves in situations that lead them closer to this eventual reality.

Exercise: Look to your dreams

- Think of that dream you wish to pursue.
- Sit down in a quiet place.
- Relax your breathing.
- Picture that dream as being attained or having happened.
- You are there in the 'picture', showing your joy.
- Feel the relevant emotions, see all the detail, hear all the sounds.
- Do whatever you can in your mind to enable you to feel it is real and attainable.
- Gradually let the picture fade.

Bring up this dream in your imagination at least two or three times a week and you'll strengthen your neural pathways so that it feels familiar. Neuroscience has now shown us that you 'rewire' your brain as you repeatedly think about certain things. The 'plasticity' of the brain sees to this.

As the dream becomes more real to you, set out on those first steps of the journey to draw you a little nearer to it. In other words, now it's time for the 'action' phase – the practice. Or you end up stuck on the starting line like most people. Nobody ever got anywhere or achieved a dream without this first phase.

You shape your *future* reality by what you do in the *present*. Look to your dreams.

Mind games

Become more aware of your perceptions with everything you think and see in life. Change your thinking, change your assumptions. Let's have a little fun as we test different aspects of your mind power:

1   Which of the two lines is the shortest?

2   A man married three women in his lifetime but insisted, when meeting other women, that he was single. He was telling the truth despite doubts from the women he met.

How is this so?

3   Take a look at the two black circles in the centre of each of the images.

Which one is bigger?

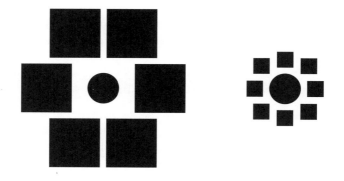

4   '_____ is more important than knowledge.'

Albert Einstein

5 A man and his son are on a hiking holiday and they both have an accident while on the cliffs. The father is taken to the clinic for minor injuries but the son is whisked over to the operating theatre. The surgeon quickly arrives on the scene and seeing the boy on the operating table says: 'I'm unable to operate on this patient – this boy is my son.'

How is this so?

6 How many triangles can you make out?

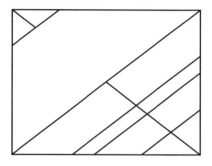

7 'Why pay a dollar for a bookmark? Why not use

_____ _____'

Steven Spielberg

See if you can fill in the two words.

8 'You're dead if you only aim for kids. Adults are only

_____ _____ _____ anyway.'

Walt Disney

See if you can fill in the three words.

9 'Disney has the best casting. If he doesn't like an actor he

just _____ _____ _____'

Alfred Hitchcock

See if you can fill in the three words.

10 Paul always lies. Richard always tells the truth. Which one of the two said, 'He claims he's Paul'?

11 Sherlock Holmes and Dr. Watson go on a camping trip. After a good dinner and a bottle of wine, they retire for the night, and go to sleep. Some hours later, Holmes wakes up and nudges his faithful friend.

'Watson, look up at the sky and tell me what you see.'

'I see millions and millions of stars, Holmes,' replies Watson.

'And what do you deduce from that?'

Watson ponders for a minute.

'Well, astronomically, it tells me that there are millions of galaxies and potentially billions of planets. Astrologically, I observe that Saturn is in Leo. Horologically, I deduce that the time is approximately a quarter past three. Meteorologically, I suspect that we will have a beautiful day tomorrow. Theologically, I can see that God is all powerful and that we are a small and insignificant part of the universe.

What does it tell you, Holmes?'

What was Sherlock Holmes' reply to Dr. Watson? (If you've heard this before, we'll call it a memory test. If you've never heard this before, we're testing your mental faculties!)

12   Now let's finally assess your intuition and/or your attention.

Take a look at the seven playing cards below. For you to win I want you to select one of the cards – the one to which you are *intuitively* drawn – and say it in your mind repeatedly. **Please do it quickly.**

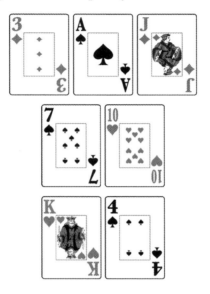

Now let's test your powers of visualisation, which you learnt about earlier on. Visualise the card and see it flying up in the air and disappearing into the clouds.

Okay – in the Appendix there are now only six cards left.

Now, if you've done your bit correctly your card will not be there. In fact I feel sure it's not there. If I'm correct and your card is not there – you win. Well done. **The winner takes it all!**

(All answers are in the Appendix, pp. 265–66.)

Coffee break . . .

 The 'winners' in life are those of us who do one thing better than most other people: win control over and use the mind so that it serves us; not the other way round.

 Much of our time is spent ruminating over internal dialogue that talks us out of doing something because we're focused on failure in some form.

 Equally, a lot of time is focused on analysing lost opportunities, with all the 'I should have' and 'I could have' statements and other forms of distorted thinking.

 The same power of thought and imagery and its self-fulfilling propensity applies to both negative and positive thought processes.

 Researchers studying the twin areas of optimism and pessimism discovered some interesting things relating to expectations. Optimists believe in and expect favourable outcomes, as opposed to *hoping* things will turn out this way. In the case of the pessimists surveyed, they expected a poor outcome.

 Attitude – which is a specific way of thinking and therefore feeling – is crucial; and attitudes are learned. We're not as helpless in the game of life as some people like to believe.

 The mind is expert at creating images – at visualising; our imaginations are very powerful. 'Distorted' thinking is pure imagination coupled with imagery.

Learning to use our imagination in a controlled way can propel us to success in all areas of life. Everything begins with a thought.

 Visualising outcomes and engaging in 'mental time travel' is a powerful way of achieving goals and dreams.

 The reason why visualisation is so powerful and effective? It creates new neural pathways of experience – even though we haven't actually *lived* the reality. Neuroscience has shown us that our thoughts alter the brain's wiring and its neurochemistry.

 The subconscious mind is key to the success of sports-people and they make extensive use of training the neural pathways in the brain by the use of visualisation.

 Many successful people, in all walks of life, make use of powerful self-talk and imagery as they adopt the process of visualisation and see their goals and dreams already fulfilled. Making the situation seem more like 'reality' eliminates distorted thinking and encourages action.

Chapter

9

'We are all in the gutter,
but some of us are looking at the stars.'

Oscar Wilde

It's a wonderful life

It's become clear by now – or rather, you have become aware – that your life up to this moment is a result of all the thoughts and beliefs you've had over the years. All of this is now what we call the past. Something we can't do anything about.

Memories of our experiences are the reminders we have of our past thoughts and feelings. All we have now – and of course it's very precious – is this 'present moment'.

It's *now* that is important for us because our beliefs and our thoughts and consequently what we say and do, is going to create our *future* life. Yet the power for this future lies in the 'now' – this present moment. It's your own mind power that will decide what kind of life you experience from now.

The way to do this, as you know, is by handling your perceptions – in other words, changing your thinking and looking at things from a different angle. Consider with whom you are making comparisons, for example – also take a look at your expectations. Remember the power of optimistic versus pessimistic thinking. We know how powerful the mind can be when we 'flick the switch' to challenge a belief.

You've seen how easy it is for the human mind to dwell on unhelpful, negative thoughts. When this mind of yours latches on to some good and positive thoughts about yourself you're quick to refute it due to some kind of 'distorted' thinking pattern (that we looked at in Chapter 2). Well, if you're capable of closing the door and refusing to think about positive thoughts, you can do the same with any negative thoughts about yourself.

As we saw earlier, 'disputing' these thoughts takes away any power from them. It gives you a new way of thinking about things. The new, different way of thinking:

- creates different feelings that;
- leads to different behaviour that;
- leads to different experiences that;
- leads to a different life.

The 'ripple effect' goes on and on.

Now that we're reaching the end of this journey that we've taken through the mind, I'd like to reiterate that it's never too late to change your thinking. Forget about how you handled things in the past. It's over. Resentment, guilt, 'I should have', 'I could have' – yes, of course it's all there as a legacy of your past thinking. Remember this:

> **You probably did the best you could** – *with the mind-set you had at the time.*

It stands to reason that you would have done some things differently if your thinking process *had* been different. But it wasn't. And it's in the past. Be aware that you can't change the past. But what you can do – which has been the message throughout *Mind Power* – is exercise the one power that you do have. The power over your thoughts.

What you thought about something in the past, say in 1970 or 1981 or 2009 (based on your *beliefs* at the time), doesn't mean that you still have to have the *same* beliefs now.

How many people have you come across who say that as a parent they now know what their own mothers and fathers went through and why they may have behaved in a certain way? Deeply held disagreements and resentments may disappear with the new-found knowledge. So they change their thoughts about the past. This changes their thinking in the present – and therefore the future.

So change your thoughts about the past. Forgive yourself for it. Analyse things that happened and your *old* thoughts about them. Look at them and remove the old 'filters' and with your new pair of eyes see whether your earlier 'distorted' thinking pattern is to blame for some of your recollections. Remember:

> **Opinions are not facts.**

If you're holding onto anger relating to people from the past (as we touched upon in Chapter 6), maybe it's time to let go. Whatever they may have done was due to some 'faulty' thinking on *their* part too. Examine the way *you* thought about things – maybe your anger with these people isn't justified. Maybe you needn't have 'fallen out' with them.

You're not necessarily saying that their behaviour was justified. You're just releasing the 'balloon with the string' and letting it go – freeing yourself. You get the benefit. When you hold on to 'toxic' thoughts you're wasting energy in this precious present moment. If you're unable to go that far with *other* people, then maybe you can do it for *yourself*.

So, what *is* this happiness in this wonderful life? The term will evoke different images for different people. Remember, it's all about perception, isn't it? Again, as the controller of your thinking, it's you who can flick the switch. Is happiness really a permanent state?

Have you ever met anybody who was happy all the time? What about those people with all that money? How short term was the happiness before they returned back to their baseline level of contentment? And those people that derive their self-esteem only from the pursuit and acquisition of more wealth. If they then lose their wealth, as you often hear about, either through deliberate squandering or bad investments – what's left?

Their money has gone and so has their self-esteem.

> **That money talks,**
> **I can't deny,**
> **I heard it once,**
> **It said, 'Goodbye.'**

Most people postpone happiness on the grounds that it will come later, sometime in the future. Yet all we ever have is the present. How often do you hear someone say that they'll be happy when they get another job, find a new girl/boyfriend, move house, lose weight, can afford an Aston Martin, win the lottery, finish an exam, write a best-seller. But of course all the time you 'wait' to be happy, you're using up this one precious moment as you put your life on hold.

Yet don't we have moments of happiness? Did you enjoy a particular meal recently? Did you see a film or a play that you enjoyed? When you were congratulated for a good piece of work by your boss, perhaps. When you saw the look on your children's faces at the fair or when you took them to see the latest *Harry Potter*. When you're at the cookery classes every week.

Think back and see if just three things come to mind that made you happy recently. You may be inclined to use a different word to describe the experience. But ultimately it probably amounts to the same feeling.

How quickly did they spring to mind? Quite quickly, I should have thought? Moments of happiness when you felt pleased or satisfied or content. And yet, if asked if you were 'happy', many of you would probably spend a lot of time in 'pause' mode before an answer. Perhaps it's the semantics. Maybe our expectations of the world lead us to feel dissatisfied, as happiness implies a constant state that we should try to attain in this life of ours.

The thing we waste most of in our lives is our life

We know though that life contains a series of moments when we're under physical or psychological stress when we're feeling overwhelmed and anxious and angry about something. We know that we can change our thinking to help us cope with these situations.

Equally, we know we can change our viewpoint to feel happier. Who said happiness can't come in 'bite-size' chunks? What about those three instances that came to your mind earlier? You were happy in the moment. **The moment is all we have.** If we postpone our happiness until a future date, what happens when you (let's take the list mentioned earlier):

- get another job;
- find a new girl/boyfriend;
- move house;
- lose weight;
- can afford an Aston Martin;
- win the lottery;
- finish exams;
- write a best-seller?

When you attain these things – sometime in the future – what *new* stresses and strains might life have thrown at you at the time of achieving the aspiration or goal?

The result: maybe you've been successful in achieving what you considered would lead you to a state of 'happiness'. Only now you've substituted a new 'I'll be happy when . . .' to take account of the present problems. What was your future has now become the new 'present' – you've got your new job, you've lost weight, but there are now a whole new set of obstacles or aspirations to deal with in the 'future'. So happiness will come 'when I . . .' And so the process continues, eating up more present moments as your distorted thinking puts your life on hold, yet again.

**'Live not as though there were a thousand years ahead of you. Fate is
at your elbow; make yourself good while life and power are still yours.'**

Marcus Aurelius

The point is this: something more is always going to come into
your 'in tray' in life to sabotage your thinking. Recognise that
in order to experience this 'wonderful life' you have to come
to terms with the fact that the elusive state of 'happiness' is
entirely a *subjective* thing. What most people are really seeking
is probably more accurately described as *contentment*. A feeling
or state that is with you *all* the time instead of single pleasurable
instances that will end, such as the triple chocolate ice-cream
sundae, the post-première party, the weekend in Paris.

Happiness is never going to be a place at which you finally
arrive. Someone once said that happiness in life can be attained
by a simple formula: *increasing* the moments of joy and *shorten-
ing* the moments of pain and discomfort. When you see people
who are happy, they tend to have a feeling about the world that
is generally positive, but there are still the emotional and mood
changes that they inevitably have to deal with.

Repeated studies show that it's the thinking 'skills' of these
people that helps them to cope when they see negativity
forming in their minds; these 'happy' people are able to spot
negativity attacking their psyche more readily than those who
are in an unhappy frame of mind. Further, they live in accord-
ance with their values, and the by-product of that is happiness.

Even though 'happy' people have these negative thoughts drift-
ing in and out of their minds, their *reaction* to the thoughts
is much healthier. They regard them as just that – merely
thoughts. Whereas people in a more negative frame of mind
regard the thoughts as *reality*, instead of cognitions that need
to be validated. So what tips do we need from those people with
healthier dispositions and an optimistic attitude to life?

Researchers have identified a number of 'constants' – the ten listed below – that are associated with people who claim to be in a state of happiness and experience an enjoyment of life:

1	Perception of being in control.
2	Optimistic.
3	Realistic expectations and goals.
4	Fitness (exercise) and good health.
5	Healthy self-esteem.
6	Outgoing personality.
7	Close relationship(s).
8	Leisure time (and hobbies).
9	Support 'system'.
10	Fulfilling work.

To repeat: the way to achieve contentment – 'happiness' – is by handling your perceptions; in other words, changing your thinking and looking at things from a different angle. 'Flick the switch' to challenge a belief. Another way, of course, is by just engaging in more pleasurable activities.

The 'past', 'present' and 'future'

We spend much of our lives living in the **past** or looking into the **future**. Regrets about the past and worry about the future stifle our 'present moment'. We have to accept that the future is uncertain. But what we mustn't lose sight of is that we can only change our future here in the present. We may not be able to change the past (we can learn from it though) but we can make sure that we plan what we do *now* – which will soon be the past – in terms of what we want to change.

Many of you may have been lucky enough to have seen the 1970 film *Scrooge*, the highly acclaimed film adaptation of Charles Dickens' *Christmas Carol* which he penned in 1843. Ebenezer Scrooge, as you're probably aware, is visited by three spirits – the Ghosts of Christmas Past, Present and Future. This is a wonderful feel-good adaptation of redemption and forgiveness and it poignantly shows how each of us has the ability to change our lives.

Scrooge: a ghostly encounter

The ghost of the future shows Scrooge his fate and that is enough for a change in his behaviour – away from material and monetary greed. He realises that he has only *one* way to change his future – by changing in the present. Scrooge suddenly finds that life is good, time is short and suddenly you are not here anymore. Realising how joyful life can be, he sets about making the present, for him and those around him, a wonderful experience. *Scrooge* is a heart-warming morality tale that teaches us a lot about how a change of thinking creates a 'ripple effect' that affects so many people. It shows how we can leave the past behind and shape the future. It's as relevant today as much as it was in the time of Charles Dickens.

*The past is **history**,*
*the future's a **mystery**,*
*but the present is a **gift**.*
That's why it's
called 'the present'

Scrooge: discovers a new outlook on life

In the same optimistic vein and with a slightly different message, is there anyone who can resist the charm of or remain untouched by Frank Capra's 1946 production, *It's A Wonderful Life?* Its message is simple but profound. Each one of us is important and has something to contribute to life. It's a film that makes you think. In fact, it's often been called 'the thinking person's film'.

It's a Wonderful Life: angelic intervention

James Stewart plays George Bailey, who sacrifices his own dreams for the sake of others in his small town of Bedford Falls. On Christmas Eve he is driven by despair to take his life but is saved by his guardian angel (Clarence Oddbody) who shows him what the world would have been like without him. George doesn't realise how much he has accomplished in life and is convinced – as he sees the 'ripple effect' of what he has contributed – of how dreary and impoverished the town would have been if he hadn't been born.

255

There's a reward for Clarence in the last scene as the young daughter tells her father, George, that when a bell rings, 'an angel gets its wings'. You can't underestimate the power, timelessness and inspiration of this film. It teaches us that life – despite the paths that we may end up taking – truly is a wonderful one. It shows that no matter how insignificant you may feel, we are all linked to each other and affect the lives of one another. The film itself is truly a life-changing experience.

It's a Wonderful Life: rediscovering the joys

We can take the morality stories from these two fine films to illustrate the fact that our lives can change when we make the effort by changing our thinking. The 'ripple effect' is at work all the time. When we change our thinking from unhealthy to good and productive thoughts, it changes our behaviour and the situations we're in, and it impacts on the people with whom we come into contact. We make a difference in life even if, like George Bailey, we haven't pursued what we wanted to do. But there's always time to change your future. Here in the present.

> **If you think you can, you can.**

So go on: change your thinking – change your life.

Coffee break . . .

 Your life up to this present is a result of all the thoughts and beliefs you've had over the years – what we call the past. Memories of those experiences is all you have.

 Our beliefs and thoughts in 'the now' are going to create our future life. It's our own mind power in the present that will decide what life experiences we have from now.

 'Disputing' thoughts takes power away from them.

 Your new way of thinking creates different feelings – that leads to different behaviour – that leads to different experiences – that leads to a different life. A 'ripple effect' that goes on and on.

 Dwelling on your past life may be counterproductive. You probably did the best you could with the *mind-set* you had at the time. You don't necessarily have the same beliefs now.

 Learn from any mistakes and shape the future. That's all you have left.

 Remember: opinions are not facts.

 To a large extent, happiness is a matter of perception. Most people postpone it until some time in the future; but all you have is **now**. 'Flick the switch.'

 The elusive state of happiness is an entirely subjective thing. Something is always going to come into your 'in tray' in life and try to sabotage your thinking. Change your thinking – what you're really seeking is contentment.

We spend most of our lives living in the past or looking to the future. We may not be able to change the past (we can learn from it) but we can change our future – but it has to happen now, in 'the present'.

 The 'ripple effect' is at work all the time. Just like the stone thrown into the water, causing ripples that affect the whole surface, we too – through a change of thinking – can alter situations that make an impact on other people and lead us to more fulfilling relationships and 'a wonderful life'.

'All art is autobiographical; the pearl is the oyster's autobiography'

Federico Fellini

Conclusion:
The art of thinking

Now we've reached the end of our odyssey into the workings of your mind. We've been down the highways, the byways and – more importantly – the *neural pathways*. It's become apparent to you now, I'm sure, that there is nothing more powerful than thought. You are what you think. The autobiography of your life begins and ends with your thinking.

Thinking is truly an art. It's not just something that happens to us, as we've seen. It's something we do. When Descartes came out with the oft-quoted phrase: '*I think; therefore I am*', of course he was right on a philosophical level. But becoming too identified with the mind is what causes us problems.

We've seen how distorted thinking takes over the mind and robs us of our power. We become identified with the whirlwind of thoughts that push us down those highways, byways and pathways that we'd rather not visit.

The problem for most of us is that we don't use our mind correctly. In fact, quite often, we don't use it at all. We become a slave to something that we should control. It uses *us*. Remember: the mind is given to us, we are not given to the mind. Make sure you etch this phrase into your mind (you're taking control of it already!) and remember it when you're having a 'tussle' with those irrational, judgmental and self-limiting thoughts that threaten to skew your behaviour.

By watching your thoughts – as we discussed in an earlier chapter – you're listening to a monologue or dialogue as an observer and at the same time *separating* yourself from your mind. Proof, if proof were needed, that you are not your mind. So, if you can observe your mind – you can control it. You have the power to stop dwelling on those negative thoughts, as you've seen. Not by suppression. But by recognising them as just thoughts, listening to them, and realising that because you have stepped back and are able to observe the thoughts – you are not your mind.

How much of our world is inhabited by people suffering, this very moment, from the 'human condition' of incessant, destructive and unhelpful chatter in their heads – that they think they're powerless to control? They have not realised that they are able to free themselves from the mind by taking the time and trouble to observe their thoughts.

Most people do not take time to *observe* thoughts – it has never occurred to them that you can actually do this. Like most of us, they were never taught how to do it. It never occurred to them that you could actually pause – like using a remote control – and look at your thinking. Schools have never been interested in teaching us what would probably be the one thing – perhaps more valuable than anything else – that would equip us best to deal with the vicissitudes in life.

History is our best teacher. What has the previous way of thinking done for our lives? Every aspect of life from health, work, finance and love will have been dependent on our thinking and the behaviour that resulted from it.

What has been the 'ripple effect' from the old, enslaved way of thinking where the mind has controlled the thinker? When we stop the 'chatter' that drains our *energy*, we can attain a state where we consciously lessen the amount of thought through observation and control and a certain amount of – stillness, or whatever other word you may wish to choose.

The mind can then be used for more creative thinking, in all aspects of the term. Great artists and inventors have spoken of achieving their ideas and inspiration at times when the mind was 'quiet'. Their 'art' was conceived through the art of thinking well.

So start today to create your destiny – your autobiography. You have the power . . . the *mind power*.

Just remember one thing. Reading about our thinking processes has probably given you a greater awareness of your mind. That is the purpose of the book. You now have to do the work and help yourself to change your way of thinking. It's time for the 'doing'. Otherwise, you'll be like the person who walked into the bookstore and said to the assistant:

'Excuse me, could you tell me where the self-help section is please?'

'I could,' she replied, 'but wouldn't that defeat the object?'

Appendix

Mind games answers

1. Aren't they both the same length? (1 point)

2. He was a priest. (1 point)

3. Aren't they the same size? (1 point)

4. Imagination. (1 point)

5. The surgeon was his mother. (Are all surgeons men?) (1 point)

6. There are 16. (1 point)

7. '... the dollar.' (1 point)

8. '... big grown-up kids.' (1 point)

9. '... tears them up.' (1 point)

10. Paul. (1 point)

11. 'Watson, you idiot! Someone has stolen our tent!' (10 points)

12.

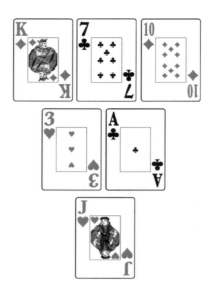

Take a look. Which card is missing? Your card isn't there, is it? The power of the mind? The power of attention? Call it what you will. Well done. (10 points)

Scoring scale:

- 10 points and above (10–30): you have the power – the *mind power*.
- Below 10 points: your mind's a blank!

Index

ALSO BY JAMES BORG

'This book is spot-on and should be a must read.'

- The Daily Telegraph

PERSUASION
The art of
influencing people

THE NUMBER ONE
BESTSELLER BY
JAMES BORG

Imagine a 'better you' who's incredibly persuasive: you charm effortlessly, you gain trust quickly, you're more influential and you win people over easily.

Think that sounds impossible? It's not. It's completely possible with *Persuasion*.

Learn the power of words; how to be an effective listener; how to develop and enhance your memory; how to control the attention of others and how to read body language and other non-verbal signs.

Persuasion will boost your persuasive and intuitive skills to amazing new levels and will help you achieve more in every area of your life.

"Persuaded? We were. Buy it."
– *Management Today* magazine

"This is a handy readable guide ... The author persuaded me to review this book. Damn, he is good."
– Jeremy Vine, *The Times*

"This book is spot-on and should be a must read."
– *The Daily Telegraph*

Buy your copy today from your favourite bookshop

eBOOK
also available

ALSO BY JAMES BORG

'Borg is an expert on body language.' – *The Times*

BODY LANGUAGE

How to know
what's REALLY being said

THE AWARD-WINNING
BESTSELLER BY
JAMES BORG

Over half of our communication is through our bodies, but how many of us know how to decipher this non-verbal language?

Body Language will make sure you get it right every time. In seven simple lessons you'll become an expert at reading others and controlling your own gestures to get the response you want.

Winner of BAA (British Airports Authority)
'Best Non-Fiction Travel Read' Award

(Voted for by the public)